COUNTRIES OF THE WORLD

Romania

Gareth Stevens Publishing
A WORLD ALMANAC EDUCATION GROUP COMPANY

About the Author: Tiberiu Oprea is a broadcast reporter for popular Romanian channel PRO TV. Trained in aerospace engineering, Oprea has ten years of experience in print and broadcast journalism. Today, she lives in Braşov.

PICTURE CREDITS

Agence France Presse: 74, 75, 78, 79, 84, 85
Art Directors & TRIP Photo Library: 2, 3 (center and bottom), 7, 8, 19 (bottom), 20, 21 (top), 25, 28 (top), 31, 33, 35, 38, 39, 40, 44, 50, 52, 53, 58, 59, 67, 68, 72, 87, 89, 91
Michele Burgess: 3 (top), 4, 13, 16, 26, 32, 66, 81
Jan Butchofsky/Houserstock, Inc.: 6, 27 (bottom)
Camera Press: 23, 83, 54, 55
Thierry Charlier/Camera Press: 77
Corbis: 47
Focus Team — Italy: 9, 27 (top), 41, 56 (top and bottom)
Getty Images/Hulton Archive: 15 (top and bottom), 36, 61, 76, 82
Bridget Gubbins: 21 (bottom), 42, 73
Haga Library, Japan: cover, 22, 43
Hepta Photo Agency: 46, 48 (top and bottom), 49, 51, 63
Dave G. Houser/Houserstock, Inc.: 18, 19 (top), 69
The Hutchison Library: 29, 45, 80
Lonely Planet Images: 70, 71
National Bank of Romania: 90
National Institute for Research and Development in Informatics: 64, 65
North Wind Picture Archives: 10, 11, 12
Pankotay/Camera Press: 17
David Rubinger/Camera Press: 14
Sonia Halliday Photographs: 5
Karen Stow/Camera Press: 28 (bottom), 57
Liba Taylor: 24
Topham Picturepoint: 60, 62
Travel Ink: 1, 30, 34
Bill Vetell/Camera Press: 37

Digital Scanning by Superskill Graphics Pte Ltd

Written by
TIBERIU OPREA

Edited by
SELINA KUO

Edited in the U.S. by
MARY DYKSTRA
LYMAN LYONS
ALAN WACHTEL

Designed by
GEOSLYN LIM

Picture research by
SUSAN JANE MANUEL

First published in North America in 2003 by
Gareth Stevens Publishing
A World Almanac Education Group Company
330 West Olive Street, Suite 100
Milwaukee, Wisconsin 53212 USA

Please visit our web site at:
www.garethstevens.com
For a free color catalog describing
Gareth Stevens Publishing's list of high-quality
books and multimedia programs, call
1-800-542-2595 (USA) or 1-800-387-3178 (Canada).
Gareth Stevens Publishing's fax: (414) 332-3567.

© **TIMES MEDIA PRIVATE LIMITED 2003**
Originated and designed by
Times Editions
An imprint of Times Media Private Limited
A member of the Times Publishing Group
Times Centre, 1 New Industrial Road
Singapore 536196
http://www.timesone.com.sg/te

Library of Congress Cataloging-in-Publication Data
Oprea, Tiberiu.
Romania / by Tiberiu Oprea.
p. cm. — (Countries of the world)
Summary: An overview of the country of Romania which includes information on geography, history, government, and social life and customs.
Includes bibliographical references and index.
ISBN 0-8368-2367-2 (lib. bdg.)
1. Romania—Juvenile literature. [1. Romania.] I. Title.
II. Countries of the world (Milwaukee, Wis.)
DR205.O67   2003
949.8—dc21   2003050408

Printed in Singapore

1 2 3 4 5 6 7 8 9 06 05 04 03

Contents

5 AN OVERVIEW OF ROMANIA

6 Geography
10 History
16 Government and the Economy
20 People and Lifestyle
28 Language and Literature
30 Arts
34 Leisure and Festivals
40 Food

43 A CLOSER LOOK AT ROMANIA

44 Bucharest
46 Călușari
48 Caves: The World Underground
50 Celebrating Junii Brașovului
52 Cleaner Living
54 Nadia Comăneci
56 Dracula
58 House of the People
60 Intellectual Life, Art, and Culture
62 Mineral Water
64 Muddy Volcanoes
66 People Power: The Revolution of 1989
68 The Roma
70 Sarmizegetusa: Ancient Ruins
72 Saving Ceaușescu's Child Victims

75 RELATIONS WITH NORTH AMERICA

For More Information …

86 Full-color map
88 Black-and-white reproducible map
90 Romania at a Glance
92 Glossary
94 Books, Videos, Web Sites
95 Index

AN OVERVIEW OF ROMANIA

Romania's geography is a rich and diverse combination of the Carpathian Mountains in the country's interior, the Black Sea to the east, and the Danube River to the south. Situated in southeastern Europe, Romania is part of the Balkan Peninsula and has been at the crossroads of Eastern and Western cultures since the Roman conquest in A.D. 106. Between the early 1300s and late 1800s, Romania existed as three separately governed states — Walachia, Moldavia, and Transylvania. These three states were officially united after World War I. Since 1989, when fifty years of communist rule came to an end, Romania has been committed to building a democratic government and moving toward greater economic stability.

Opposite: **The former Boulevard of Socialist Victory in Bucharest leads to the Palace of Parliament, formerly called the House of the People. The Palace is the world's second-largest building, after the Pentagon in Washington, D.C.**

Below: **Romania is slowly emerging from a heavily agricultural past.**

THE FLAG OF ROMANIA

The tricolor Romanian flag features sections of blue, yellow, and red from left to right. A coat of arms was once positioned in the middle of the yellow band, but is no longer there today. The flag of Romania, similar to the flags of many European states, was inspired by the spirit and success of the French revolution in the eighteenth century. The origin of the colors in the flag, however, is uncertain. Some accounts claim the three colors were part of fifteenth- and sixteenth-century battle flags raised during wars waged against the invading Ottoman Turks and Hungarians.

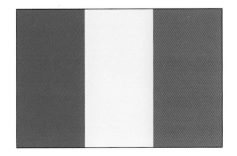

Geography

Romania covers an area of about 91,675 square miles (237,500 square kilometers) and is bordered by Ukraine to the north and east, Moldova to the northeast, the Black Sea to the southeast, Bulgaria to the south, Serbia and Montenegro to the southwest, and Hungary to the northwest.

Mountains and Plains

Romania's area includes mountains, hills, and plains. From the Ukrainian border in the north, the Eastern Carpathian Mountains extend southeast into Romania before turning west to form the Transylvanian Alps, which are also known as the Southern Carpathians. Part of the Transylvanian Alps, Mount Moldoveanu is the country's highest point at 8,347 feet (2,544 meters). The hills of the Transylvanian Plateau lie in the arc formed by the Carpathian ranges.

The hills, plateaus, and plains of the Moldavia region extend east from the mountains toward the Prut River at Romania's eastern border with Moldova. Likewise, hills, plateaus, and plains extend south through the Walachia region to the Danube River at the southern border with Bulgaria.

BUCHAREST

The capital of Romania, Bucharest was founded in 1459. Once nicknamed "Little Paris of the East," the city has since lost much of its former glory.
(A Closer Look, page 44)

MUDDY VOLCANOES

In Buzău county, the Eastern Carpathians curve westward into the Transylvanian Alps. Quaint land formations described as "muddy volcanoes" dot the landscape in this region.
(A Closer Look, page 64)

THE BLACK SEA

Romania's coastline along the Black Sea (*left*) measures about 140 miles (225 km) long. The Black Sea lies at sea level and is Romania's lowest point. Dobruja is a small region between the Black Sea and the Danube River in the southeastern part of Romania.

Walachia is the country's main agricultural region. Where the Danube River turns north and flows through Romania, the low-lying Dobruja region lies between the river and the Black Sea. The Tisza Plain covers the area west of the Carpathians and is usually recognized as two smaller regions: Banat and Crisana-Maramureş. Banat is the southern half of the Tisza Plain, which borders Serbia and Montenegro, while Crisana-Maramureş is the northern half, which lies closer to Hungary.

Above: **The Danube Delta, which is the region where the mouth of the Danube River meets the Black Sea, covers much of northeastern Dobruja.**

Rivers and Lakes

Romania's border with Bulgaria is marked by the Danube River, which empties into the Black Sea. The Danube flows for a total of 1,771 miles (2,850 kilometers), including about 668 miles (1,075 km) in Romania. Most of the country's other major rivers, including the Mureş, Olt, Prut, Siret, and Someş rivers, are tributaries of the Danube.

Romania is home to more than 2,300 lakes. Lake Razelm, which covers an area of about 160 square miles (415 sq km), is Romania's largest lake.

CAVES: THE WORLD UNDERGROUND

Romania is home to more than 12,000 caves. The Movile Cave near the Black Sea is probably the most famous.
(A Closer Look, page 48)

7

Left: **In February 2003, temperatures in the mountainous counties of Covasna, Harghita, and Braşov dipped to an unusually cold -4° F (-20° C).**

Climate

Romania's climate is a combination of temperate and continental conditions, with four distinct seasons in each year. Romanian winters are typically cold, snowy and cloudy, while summers are mostly sunny, with frequent showers and occasional thunderstorms. Because of Romania's position on the European continent, the climate in eastern, and especially southeastern, Romania tends to be more continental. The climate in central and western Romania is generally more temperate, or without extremes in temperature. Altitude, however, creates variations in temperatures during the same season. Temperatures are always cooler in the mountains and warmer in low-lying regions, such as Walachia, Moldavia, and Dobruja. In Bucharest, summer temperatures range between 61° and 86° Fahrenheit (16° and 30° Celsius), while winter temperatures range between 19° and 34° F (-7° and 1° C).

Romania's rainiest months occur from April to June and from September to October. The country receives an annual average of about 25 inches (635 millimeters) of rainfall, with the mountainous regions receiving twice the amount of rain received in the plains. Dobruja, which has an annual average of about 16 inches (406 mm) of rainfall, is Romania's driest region.

Plants and Animals

Forests cover about 25 percent of Romania. The lower slopes of the country's mountainous interior, at elevations of up to about 4,600 feet (1,402 m), are typically covered by deciduous trees such as oaks and beeches. Higher in the mountains, between 4,600 and 5,900 feet (1,402 and 1,798 m), forested areas mostly consist of coniferous trees such as pines and spruces. Above 5,900 feet (1,798 m), subalpine and alpine vegetation become increasingly visible. Most of the wooded plains in Walachia and Moldavia have been cleared for human settlement and agriculture. Fruit trees thrive near the foothills of Romania's numerous mountains.

The treasure of Romania's rich animal life is the rare chamois, a small goatlike antelope with straight horns that bend backward at the tips. Chamois are found high in the Carpathian Mountains. Romania's forests are home to a wide variety of wildlife, including brown bears, red deer, wolves, foxes, wild pigs, lynx, and various songbirds. Because of the country's many rivers, lakes, and the Black Sea, aquatic life in Romania also is diverse. Pike, sturgeon, flounder, herring, salmon, perch, and eel are plentiful in Romania.

Below: **The Danube Delta in southeastern Romania is home and host to a great many species of birds.**

History

Origin of the Dacians

Around 2000 B.C., migratory Indo-European tribes, the Thracians, arrived in the region that is now Romania. In the seventh century B.C., descendants of the Thracians first came into contact with Greek peoples, who had moved to the western shore of the Black Sea. By the fifth century B.C., the Greeks knew the various tribes of the Romanian region collectively as Getae. The Romans later called them Dacians and their land Dacia.

The Romans and the Slavs

In the first century B.C., the Romans advanced into the Balkan Peninsula and disrupted Dacian life. The Romans, however, did not conquer the Dacians until A.D. 106. The Transylvanian Plateau and the Walachian Plains then became Dacia, a province of the Roman Empire, until A.D. 271, when the Romans officially withdrew from the region.

For nearly 800 years after it was abandoned by the Romans, Dacia was successively conquered by migratory peoples. Most notably, in A.D. 567, the Avars defeated the ruling Germanic Gepidae, and their victory led to a wave of Slavs entering Dacia. Although the Slavs controlled Dacia, they were vastly outnumbered by the Romanized Dacians, who eventually assimilated the Slavs. Over the centuries, a distinct, Latin-

SARMIZEGETUSA: ANCIENT RUINS

The Dacians had a developed society and culture by 1000 B.C. Today, ruins of the Dacian capital and fortresses, as well as Roman towns, can be seen at Sarmizegetusa, a historical site near the present-day city of Hunedoara.

(A Closer Look, page 70)

Below: **During Roman rule, goverment officials, soldiers, and traders entered Dacia. These new settlers brought with them the influence of Roman administration and the use of the Latin language. They also built several new cities.**

speaking ethnic group formed. The members of this group were the early ancestors of ethnic Romanians.

The Hungarians and the Ottoman Turks

In the tenth century, the Hungarians swept into Dacia and destablized the region. By the early eleventh century, Hungary had claimed the Transylvanian Plateau, where centuries of Hungarian domination spurred many Romanians to emigrate farther south or east. The independent principalities of Walachia and Moldavia were formed in 1330 and 1359, respectively.

In the 1400s, the Ottoman Turks advanced into southeastern Europe. The two principalities remained largely autonomous by capitulating to the Turks, who demanded little more than a yearly tax on goods, such as grain and timber, and official acknowledgement of the Ottoman ruler. In 1526, the Turks crushed the Hungarians in a battle at Mohács, and Hungarian territory was divided into western, central, and eastern thirds by 1541. Beginning then and continuing for most of the 1600s, eastern Hungary, which included Transylvania, was ruled by Hungarian nobility under an agreement with the Turks. The Turks retreated from Hungary in 1686 but remained in Walachia and Moldavia until 1878.

The Austrians and the Russians

In 1699, the Hapsburgs of Austria succeeded the rule of the Ottoman Turks in Hungary, but the lives of Romanians in Transylvania did not improve. As before, Romanians in Transylvania were excluded from public life and privileges mainly because most of them were peasants and Orthodox Christians. In 1867, the dual monarchy of Austria and Hungary monarchy was formed, and Transylvania again came under direct Hungarian rule.

The Russians became prominent in Romanian history after 1774, when Russia promised to protect all Orthodox Christians in the Ottoman Empire under the Treaty of Küçük Kaynarca. In return, the Romanians supported the Russians in their fight against the Ottoman Turks. By 1829, the Russians had control of Walachia and Moldavia even though they were still formally Ottoman territories. In 1848, a group of revolutionaries campaigned for Romanian independence but were quashed by a Russian army sent to Bucharest. Russia's domination waned after it lost the Crimean War (1853–1856).

In 1859, Alexandru Cuza was elected the sole ruler of both Moldavia and Walachia and began sweeping reforms to develop the principalities as one nation. By 1866, a new constitution was adopted and the principalities unofficially became known as Romania. In 1878, Romania gained formal independence.

Left: This artwork depicts Bucharest when it was the capital of Walachia (1659–1862). After Alexandru Cuza took power in 1859, he united Walachia and Moldavia. He also moved to secularize the newly formed country by introducing laws that reduced the influence of the Orthodox clergy in civil matters. In 1866, Prince Carol of Hohenzollern-Sigmaringen, who later became King Carol I (r.1881–1914), succeeded Cuza.

The Two World Wars

Romania entered World War I with a new king, Ferdinand I. When the war began in 1914, Romania declared a policy of neutrality. By 1916, however, Romania entered the conflict and fought against Germany and Austria-Hungary. When the war ended with the Allies victorious, Romania gained Transylvania from Hungary; Bessarabia (in present-day Moldova) from Russia; and Bukovina, a region covering present-day northern Romania and southwestern Ukraine, from Austria-Hungary.

For most of the 1920s, Romania developed a democratic government and a somewhat prosperous economy. In the 1930s, the Romanian government began to align itself with Nazi Germany, but the signing of a German-Soviet nonagression pact in 1939 led Romania to lose the bulk of its postwar territorial gains.

Romania fought on the side of Germany when World War II began and, in 1941, reclaimed Bukovina and took southeastern Ukraine from the Soviets. In 1944, after the Soviet army dealt a crushing blow to the Romanians and entered Bucharest, Romania switched sides and declared war on Germany. In 1945, the Soviet Union pressured Romania into installing a procommunist government, which was led by Petru Groza.

Above: **The Arch of Triumph in Bucharest commemorates Romania's victory in World War I.**

THE IRON GUARD

In 1927, King Ferdinand I died, sparking renewed unrest in the country. By 1929, a worldwide recession had caused many Romanians to become unemployed, and they lost confidence in the democratic government as a result. Fascist groups then grew in number and strength. In 1940, the Iron Guard, the most powerful group, overthrew the Romanian monarchy and positioned General Ion Antonescu to become dictator. Antonescu led Romania to defeat in World War II.

PEOPLE POWER: THE REVOLUTION OF 1989

On December 15, 1989, what started as a relatively minor protest in the city of Timişoara snowballed into a nationwide uprising. One week later, Nicolae Ceauşescu (*left*) and his wife, Elena (*right*), were arrested. They were executed on Christmas day.
(*A Closer Look, page 66*)

SOVIETIZATION

Beginning in 1948 and continuing through the 1950s, nearly all aspects of Romanian life were modeled on Soviet examples. The Romanian Communist Party held supreme power in the government. Agriculture and heavy industry were favored in the development of the economy, and artistic or academic works were only permitted if they promoted communist principles. The *Securitate* (SEH-KOO-ree-TAH-teh), a secret police force set up by the Communist Party, monitored the country for dissidents during this time. In keeping with Soviet foreign policy, Romania became a member of the Council for Mutual Economic Assistance (COMECON) in 1949 and the Warsaw Pact in 1955.

The Communist Years and After

On December 30, 1947, the People's Republic of Romania was founded. Earlier that year, northern Transylvania was returned to Romania. Gheorghe Gheorghiu-Dej, leader of the Romanian Communist Party since 1945, succeeded Groza in 1952 and remained loyal to the Soviet Union until Nikita Khrushchev succeeded Joseph Stalin. Khrushchev wanted to downgrade Romania's economy to that of a supplier of agricultural goods and raw materials for other industry-focused countries in the Warsaw Pact. In 1965, Gheorghiu-Dej died, and Nicolae Ceauşescu succeeded him.

Ceauşescu reestablished dictatorial rule in the country. By the 1980s, he had turned Romania into a police state and what has been described as a "personality cult." The country's governing institutions were run by members of his family, who did whatever he desired. In 1989, Ceauşescu's regime crumbled, and the National Salvation Front, headed by Ion Iliescu, took control. Iliescu was elected president in May 1990. Since then, Romanian government has been democratic. In 2002, Romania was welcomed into the North Atlantic Treaty Organization (NATO) as a full member.

Stephen the Great (1435–1504)

Stephen the Great (r. 1457 to 1504) came to power with the help of Vlad Ţepeş — more famously known as Vlad the Impaler — who was the prince of Walachia at that time. Throughout his reign, Stephen defended against multiple invasions by the Ottoman Turks, the Hungarians, and later the Poles. Stephen's sustained resistance effort against the Turks won the praise of Pope Sixtus IV, who called him the "Athlete of Christ." Today, Stephen is recorded in Romanian history books as a fearless defender of Christianity and the Romanian people.

Michael the Brave (1558–1601)

Michael the Brave became prince of Walachia in 1593. His ambition led him to conquer Transylvania in October 1599 and Moldavia in May 1600, when he became the first leader in history to unite the three main territories of modern Romania. Although short-lived, this unification is recognized as the beginnings of Romania as a nation.

King Carol I

King Carol I (1839–1914)

King Carol I (r. 1881–1914) is remembered as the leader who secured Romania's independence from the Ottoman Turks. He first ruled Romania as Prince Carol (r. 1866–1881), and during this time, he trained the Romanian army to become powerful. With Russian support, he later led the army to victory in Romania's War of Independence (1877–1878) against the Turks. In May 1881, Carol was crowned King Carol I. His wife, Elizabeth, was a famous poetess of the time and wrote under the pseudonym Carmen Sylva.

Queen Marie

Queen Marie (1875–1938)

The granddaughter of Queen Victoria of Great Britian and Tsar Alexander II of Russia, Marie of Saxa-Coburg-Gotha married Ferdinand, the nephew and heir of King Carol I, in 1893. Famous for her charm and intelligence, she is fondly remembered by the Romanian people as a loyal patron of the arts, a selfless nurse during World War I, and a shrewd politician who negotiated Romania's postwar territorial gains.

Government and the Economy

A Democratic Republic

The Romanian government consists of three main branches: executive, legislative, and judicial. The executive branch is led by the president, who is elected by the people to serve a four-year term. The president appoints the prime minister, who in turn appoints members of the cabinet, called the Council of Ministers. In 2000, Ion Iliescu won the presidential election and appointed Adrian Nastase to serve as prime minister.

The legislative branch, called the Parliament, is divided into the Senate (143 seats), or the upper house, and the Chamber of Deputies (343 seats), or the lower house. Members of both houses are elected by the people to serve four-year terms.

Romania's judicial branch consists of the Supreme Court of Justice and a system of lower courts, including county, local, and military courts. Members of the Superior Council of Magistrates, who are elected by the Romanian parliament to serve four-year terms, recommend potential members of the Supreme Court of Justice to the president, who appoints them.

PROPORTIONAL REPRESENTATION

Members of both houses of parliament are elected based on a system of proportional representation. Under this system, each administrative region is given a number of seats based on the total number of votes cast by the people of the region. The given seats are then divided between the political parties in each administrative region based on the number of votes they won. All Romanians eighteen years of age and older are eligible to vote.

Local Government

Romania is divided into forty-two administrative regions, which consist of forty-one counties, or *judete* (joo-DEH-TSE), and the municipality of Bucharest. Administratively, the Romanian government regards the municipality of Bucharest as a county. Each county exercises local autonomy and is led by a *prefect* (pre-FEHKT). Romania's counties are divided into 260 towns. Romania's towns are further split into more than 2,680 communes.

The Military

Romania's military consist of the Army, Navy, Air and Air Defense Forces, Paramilitary Forces, Civil Defense, and Border Guards. All male Romanians must perform military service, which can last from one year to eighteen months, when they are twenty years old. In 2002, more than 5.9 million Romanians were statistically available for military service, but only about 4.9 million were considered suitably fit. Nearly 180,000 men reach military age in Romania each year. In 2002, Romania's military spending amounted to about U.S. $985 million, which is about 2.5 percent of Romania's gross domestic product (GDP).

Above: In December 1989, Romanian soldiers who were initially loyal to Ceauşescu turned against him and joined protesters in bringing down his regime.

Opposite: Romanian parliamentary sessions are held in the former headquarters of the Romanian Communist Party Central Committee. The building was known as the House of the People during communist rule.

A Struggling Economy

Since the fall of communism, the Romanian government has faced the uphill task of guiding the country toward a free-market economy. Because Romania's industrial sector was largely outdated, it was unattactive to foreign investors, which slowed the government's initial attempts to privatize state-owned enterprises. With support from the International Monetary Fund (IMF) during the period between October 2001 and March 2003, however, the Romanian government was able to take serious steps toward reforming the country's economy. These steps included extensive privatization, reducing national debt, and slowing inflation.

The latest available figures state that Romania had a workforce of nearly 10 million people in 1999, with 40 percent of its workers in agriculture, 25 percent in industry, and 35 percent in the service industry. In 2000, 55 percent of the country's gross domestic product (GDP) was earned by the service sector, while industry (30 percent) and agriculture (15 percent) provided the remaining 45 percent of the GDP. In 2001, the rate of inflation in Romania was estimated at 34.5 percent, while the unemployment rate was about 9 percent. In view of rising inflation, the near future appears grim for many Romanians. More than 44 percent already lived below the poverty line in 2000.

Above: **Romania sells most of its exports to Italy, Germany, and France. It gets most of its imports from the same countries.**

CLEANER LIVING

Many Romanians today are coping with the extensive water and air pollution caused by industrialization during the communist and Ceauşescu years. In early 2000, ill-equipped Romanian operations caused two separate industrial accidents that devastated the Danube River system. The postcommunist government has been working hard to improve the country's dismal environmental situation. Progress, although slow, has been steady.
(A Closer Look, page 52)

Agriculture

Over 40 percent of Romania's land is farmed, and Romanian farmers mainly grow wheat, corn, sugar beets, potatoes, and grapes. The Black Sea and the Danube are rich sources of fish for food. Caviar, the eggs of sturgeon, is also an important product. Forests cover over one-fourth of the country and most are state-owned. Timber derived from Romanian forests is used to support other industries, such as paper and furniture making.

Industry

Romania's industrial sector mainly consists of manufacturing and mining. Coal, iron ore, bauxite, copper, lead, and zinc are the country's main mining products. Romania's mining industry was once dominated by crude oil, but reserves have been depleted. A legacy of the communist era, Romania's manufacturing sector in the 1990s produced machinery; chemicals; cement and other construction materials; and iron, steel, and wood products. Relatively few consumer goods, such as textiles, clothing, footwear, and processed food, were produced.

TOURISM

The tourism industry has become the key feature of Romania's service sector since communism fell in 1989. Tourists from around the world visit Romania to experience the magnificence of the Carpathian Mountains and the rich ecosystem of the Danube Delta. Increasingly, tourists pamper themselves at one of the country's many luxurious spas.

Below: The Murfatlar vineyards in the Dobruja region are some of the best in the country. Viticulture, the growing of grapes and grapevines, is a significant industry in Romania.

People and Lifestyle

A Declining Population

In 2002, Romania had a population of more than 22.3 million people. A census conducted ten years earlier, however, reported a population of more than 22.8 million people. Falling birth rates and rising emigration rates were two causes of Romania's population decline. Today, 68.8 percent of Romanians are between fifteen and sixty-four years of age. Romanians aged fourteen or younger form 17.4 percent of the population, while Romanians sixty-five and older make up 13.8 percent.

According to 1992 figures, ethnic Romanians formed a vast majority of the country's population, at 89.5 percent. The remaining 10.5 percent consisted of Hungarians (7.1 percent), Roma (1.8 percent), Germans (0.5 percent), Ukrainians (0.3 percent), and a handful of other minority groups (0.8 percent), including Serbs, Croats, Russians, Turks, and Tatars. In Romania, most Hungarians and Germans live in Transylvania, with most Turks and Tatars living in Dobruja. Eighteen minority ethnic groups are officially recognized in Romania, and each group is represented in the Romanian parliament.

Above: **Two ethnic Hungarian boys from the village of Szek in Transylvania pose in their traditional clothes. Romanians call their village "Sic."**

THE ROMA

The Roma, or Gypsies, are often described as a wandering, or nomadic, people even though many have had permanent residences for generations. Romanian Roma have suffered immense discrimination because of their ethnicity in the past. The postcommunist government has taken serious steps toward improving the lives of Roma in the country.
(*A Closer Look, page 68*)

Left: **Romanian women tend to outlive men, who live an average of sixty-seven years. Romanian women live an average of about seventy-four years.**

The Urban-Rural Divide

Lifestyles in Romania's urban and rural regions differ significantly, and differences in traditional and religious values play a large part in creating the gap. Urban Romanians, for example, have many opportunities to meet and socialize with members of the opposite sex. In rural regions, strict cultural laws govern the way men and women interact. In some villages, the only way men and women meet is via the *Hora* (hoh-RAW), a traditional folk dance.

Although most Romanians have both civil and religious marriages, many rural Romanians regard the civil marriage as a legal formality and only live with their partners after the religious ceremony has been conducted. Marriages ending in divorce are rare in rural Romania.

The staunch, traditional values that dominate the culture in rural Romania have even led some to refuse modern technology. For example, washing machines are frowned upon in many villages because women who use them are regarded as antisocial and lazy. Many rural families also refuse to use refrigerators, opting to preserve food in more traditional ways.

Above: **Rural Romanian boys pose with their homemade wooden carts. The Romanian population is divided between the country's urban and rural areas, with 55 percent of Romanians estimated to be living in urban areas and 45 percent in rural areas. Romania's most populated cities include Bucharest, Constanța, Iași, Timișoara, Cluj-Napoca, Galați, Brașov, and Craiova.**

Family Life

Romanians generally maintain strong family ties, and children are considered important to a marriage. The basic family unit typically consists of a couple and their unmarried children. Aside from the Roma, few Romanians now have more than two children.

Because it is compulsory for all Romanian men to undergo military training between the ages of twenty and twenty-one, many choose not to marry until they have completed their military service. City dwellers tend to marry later in life than their rural counterparts. In the past, it was not uncommon for married children to live with their parents, but more and more newlywed couples are choosing to start their own households. Some Romanians live with their extended families, which typically include grandparents. Elderly Romanians are often cared for by their grown children. Older Romanians who live in nursing homes usually have no children or close relatives to provide care for them. Gender equality in the home is generally practiced, although some rural households remain male-dominated. Usually, both parents play active roles in bringing up children, and decisions relating to the home and family life are discussed and reached together.

Below: **A newlywed couple poses for a photograph during their traditional wedding celebration.**

Women in Romania

Making up about half of the Romanian workforce, women are usually employed in the manufacturing, education, and health sectors. Few, however, hold managerial positions. Romanian women living in rural areas are predominantly engaged in agricultural activities. Women are also expected to perform domestic chores and raise the children.

Since 1989, the Romanian government has worked to improve the status of women in the workplace through the passage of laws that protect female employees. These laws prohibit discrimination by employers with regard to gender and protect women from harassment in the workplace. In 1998, the National Plan for Action for Equal Opportunities between Men and Women was established. In spite of this progress, women still tend to earn less than their male counterparts.

In recent years, female representation in the Romanian government has gradually increased. Following the national and local elections of 2000, women made up 10.7 percent and 5.7 percent of the Senate and Chamber of Deputies, respectively. Women, however, remain underrepresented in the political arena.

SAVING CEAUŞESCU'S CHILD VICTIMS

Romania's high number of orphans can be attributed to the policies of Nicolae Ceauşescu. In an attempt to boost the Romanian population and, therefore, economic growth, married women were required to have at least five children. As a direct result of this policy, the country's orphanages swelled with children — sometimes called Ceauşescu's children — abandoned by parents who were too poor to raise them.

(A Closer Look, page 72)

HARDEST HIT

Until 1989, the government provided many child-care centers, enabling women to continue working after having children. Today, however, the number of government-run child-care facilities has declined, and parents are now expected to pay for child care. As a result, more women are forced to stay at home because they cannot afford to pay the high fees. In addition, the country's economic reforms since 1989 have led to high levels of unemployment, and women are usually the first to lose their jobs. Research has also shown that women are more likely to live at the poverty level, with four-fifths of single-parent households in Romania headed by women.

Education

The Romanian educational system is divided into three main levels: primary school, secondary school, and university. Romanians between the ages of seven and fourteen must attend school for eight years, and education is free. Primary, or elementary, school education lasts four years (grades one through four). Lower secondary school lasts another four years, through grade eight.

Secondary school, or high school, lasts for four years (grades nine through twelve) and is free but not compulsory. Romanian students can choose to enter one of five types of secondary schools run by the Ministry of Education: general education, vocational, art, physical education, and teacher-training schools.

Romanian is not always the language of instruction in the country's schools. Some students, especially those belonging to minorities, are schooled entirely in foreign languages such as German and Hungarian. The cultural and linguistic differences of minorities such as Hungarians and Roma are recognized by the government and protected under Romanian laws.

Below: **Romania has a literacy rate of about 97 percent. Slightly more men than women are able to read and write. In recent years, the Romanian Ministry of Education has launched programs aimed at educating illiterate Romanians who are over the age of twenty-five.**

Higher Education

Romania has dozens of public and private universities, with the latter emerging only after communism fell in the country in 1989. Romania's two oldest universities are the University of Bucharest and the Al I. Cuza University. Located in Iaşi, the Al I. Cuza University was founded in 1860, while the University of Bucharest was founded in 1694. The Babes-Bolyai University in Cluj-Napoca is the next oldest, with a history that dates back to 1919. Some universities, such as the University of Craiova, founded in 1966, were developed from polytechnic, or technical, colleges.

Only a percentage of students in public universities receive a free or government-subsidized education. The remaining students, as well as those in private universities, are required to pay full fees, which can be costly. Basic degree programs range from four to six years depending on the field of study. Medicine, law, economics, political science, and information technology are among the more popular areas of study. Student-exchange programs, which typically last one or two semesters, are also popular with Romanian undergraduates.

Above: Romania's oldest university, the University of Bucharest has a history that dates back to the late seventeenth century.

Christianity

Romania is a predominantly Christian country, with more than 80 percent of the population practicing a form of the religion. The Romanian Christian community, however, is split into many different groups, which range from Catholics to Protestants to Orthodox Christians.

About 70 percent of the country's population are loyal to the Romanian Orthodox Church, which is an independent branch of the Eastern Orthodox Church. Followers recognize the patriarch, or chief bishop, of Romania as head of the church.

In contrast, the Catholics regard the pope, or the bishop of Rome, as the head of the church. Six percent of Romanians are Catholics, split about equally into two groups: Uniate Catholics and Roman Catholics. What separates the two today are mainly their acts of worship, as well as slightly different doctrines. While the Roman Catholics follow the more universal Latin rites, the Uniate Catholics practice Eastern Orthodox traditions. Ethnically, most Roman Catholics in the country are of German

Above: **The Catedrala Patriarhala, or Patriarchal Cathedral, in Bucharest was built in the seventeenth century. Romanian national hero King Carol I, then Prince Carol, and his wife, then known as Princess Elizabeth of Wied, were crowned king and queen in the cathedral in 1881.**

Opposite: **The Voroneţ convent for nuns was built by Stephen the Great in the 1400s.**

or Hungarian descent and are concentrated in Transylvania. In the 1200s, Hungarian king Béla IV sent groups of Saxons and other Germanic peoples to Transylvania to fortify Hungarian dominance in the region. Roman Catholicism in Transylvania was later upheld by the ruling Austrians.

About 6 percent of Romanians are Protestant. Other denominations represented in the country include Baptists, Presbyterians, Pentecostalists, and Jehovah's Witnesses. Ethnic Hungarians and Germans who are Protestant tend to belong to Lutheran or Calvinist churches.

Minority Faiths

Of the remaining 18 percent of Romanians, the vast majority are unaffiliated with any religion. Some Turks and Tatars practice Islam, and a small number of Jewish Romanians still reside in the country today. Romania once had a significant Jewish population, especially after the first half of the 1800s, when immigrants from Russia and Poland poured into the country. Most Jewish Romanians, however, have since emigrated, and many synagogues in the country have been converted into Christian churches.

Above: **This mosque is located in Constanţa. Since the collapse of the communist regime in 1989, Romanians have enjoyed religious freedom, which is guaranteed by the 1991 constitution.**

CĂLUŞARI

The *Căluşari* (CAH-loo-shaah-ree) are a mystical religious group that was once dominant in southern Romania. The group's religious practices and doctrines are mostly secret; no one knows for certain when or how the traditions of the Căluşari first arose. The earliest recorded mention of the Căluşari dates back to the seventeenth century, when Romanian nobleman Dimitrie Cantemir described them in his writings about the history, politics, and culture of the Romanian people. The dance of the Căluşari is probably the most famous of their traditions. (*A Closer Look, page 46*)

Language and Literature

A Romance Language

Romanian is the official language of Romania. Also known as Daco-Romanian, Romanian has been classified as a Romance language, which means it was derived from Latin. Italian, Spanish, and French are other Romance languages.

Romanian has three little-used dialects: Aromanian, Istro-Romanian, and Megleno-Romanian. The latter two are nearly extinct. Aromanian, however, is still spoken by isolated communities in Greece, Yugoslavia, Albania, and Bulgaria.

Similar to other Romance languages, the majority of Romanian words originated from Latin. Despite their shared Latin roots, however, the Romanian language developed differently from other Romance languages. Because Romania was geographically closer to speakers of Slavic languages and Hungarian than its linguistic cousins, the Romanian language came to adopt some Slavonic and Hungarian words. Turkish words also crept into the Romanian vocabulary during the centuries of Ottoman rule.

INTELLECTUAL LIFE, ART, AND CULTURE

Romanian art, culture, and intellectualism developed considerably in the period between World Wars I and II. Among the people whose works contributed to this period of growth are theologian Mircea Eliade, playwright Eugène Ionesco, writer Emil Cioran, and Georges Enesco, a gifted violinist and composer.

(A Closer Look, page 60)

Left: Founded in 1866, the Romanian Academy is an important institution of academic research. The academy's library contains more than seven million publications.

Left: **In 1508, the first book, although in Slavic, was printed in Walachia. The first book in Romanian, a translation, was printed in 1559. For the next century, books in Romanian were always translations and consisted mostly of religious texts and some secular texts.**

Literature

The late 1600s was a period of notable Romanian literary achievements, which included the publication of the first poetry written in Romanian in 1673 and a translation of the Bible in 1688. In the 1700s, Ienăchiţă Văcărescu compiled the first grammar of Romanian, while his son, Alecu, helped promote lyric poetry. Alecu's son, Iancu, in turn was an exceptional poet and became known as the father of Romanian poetry.

Modern Romanian literature first took shape in the 1800s. Grigore Alexandrescu is famous for his collections of fables and satires and is revered as one of Romania's greatest writers of the Romantic era. The creation of modern Romanian poetry has been attributed to Mihail Eminescu, who was influenced by Hindu and German ways of thinking. Eminescu also wrote essays and short stories.

Twentieth-century Romanian literature was mainly an extension of nineteenth-century literary traditions, including lyric poetry and plays. After the two world wars, however, more and more writers began to write realistically about their surroundings and day-to-day life. Zaharia Stancu and Eusebiu Camilar are two such Romanian authors. Stancu wrote of village life in his novels, while Camilar heavily criticized fascism.

DRACULA

Today, Bram Stoker's novel *Dracula* enjoys a reputation around the world as a literary classic. The novel's notorious main character was inspired by the life of Vlad Ţepeş, who ruled the principality of Walachia in the 1400s. Ţepeş was a fierce defender of Romanian land and identity, and he waged bloody wars against the invading Ottoman Turks.

(A Closer Look, page 56)

Arts

Religious Architecture

Romania is home to a rich collection of religious buildings with both historical and architectural significance. In Moldavia, Stephen the Great and Prince Petru Rares built numerous monasteries in the 1400s and 1500s. The monasteries were a blend of Byzantine architecture and Gothic decorative influences. Some monasteries, including Putna and Voroneţ, were later richly decorated with paintings on both the interior and exterior walls. Today, these monasteries are located in the county of Suceava, an area previously known as southern Bukovina, and are treasured as fine examples of Moldavian art and architecture. In Walachia, sixteenth- and seventeenth-century religious buildings, including the Dealu, Snagov, and Hurez monasteries and the Episcopal Church, were distinguished from their contemporaries by their structural complexities and intricate ornamentation. In Transylvania, the period of Roman Catholic dominance introduced Western European tastes to the region. Touches of Renaissance and, later, Baroque designs became apparent in architecture after the medieval years.

Above: **Painstakingly intricate paintings adorn the exterior and interior walls of some Moldavian monasteries in northern Romania.**

HOUSE OF THE PEOPLE

Dictator Nicolae Ceauşescu destroyed far more than what he built in Bucharest. Today, the Romanian parliament building, formerly known as the House of the People, stands in central Bucharest and is an imposing reminder of Ceauşescu's self-serving architectural vision.
(A Closer Look, page 58)

Left: **The Three Hierarchs Church in Iaşi was built in the seventeenth century.**

Above: **Built in 1953, the National Opera House in Bucharest can seat about one thousand music lovers.**

Theater

Based on archaeological remains, there is reason to believe that theater in Romania has a history dating back to Dacian times, when performances would have been staged in an open-air arena. It was not until 1817, however, that the Oravita Theater opened and staged the first performances in the Romanian language. The Arad Theater opened the following year. From then until the mid-1800s, Romanian theater flourished. Many theaters opened and many more theater groups, including the Literary Society (1827) and the Philharmonic and Drama Conservatory of Iaşi (1836), formed within a short span of time. The Iaşi Theater opened in 1848, and the Bucharest Theater, which could seat about one thousand people, opened four years later. By 1996, Romania had fifty-two theaters. The number of theatergoers in the country peaked in the 1980s, when as many as 6 to 7 million Romanians attended plays. Famous Romanian playwrights include Dimitrie Bolintineanu (1825–1872), Mihai Eminescu (1850–1889), I. L. Caragiale (1852–1912), and Eugène Ionesco (1909–1994). Although Romanian-born, Ionesco was educated in Paris and wrote in French.

Folk Songs and Music

Song and dance figure prominently in Romania's folk culture. In fact, a song exists for just about every aspect of rural Romanian life. Romanians sing during major events, such as weddings and funerals; religious ceremonies, such as rain dances or exorcisms, or celebrations, such as Christmas or Easter. Village women sing when they work on communal projects and also at the end of the working day, when they gather to relax and unwind.

Apart from songs, Romania's folk music culture also includes instrumental tunes, with the violin, the *cobză* (cob-ZAH), and the *ţambal* (tsaam-BAAL) being some of the key instruments. The cobză is a stringed instrument similar to a lute, while the ţambal resembles a cross between a guitar and a xylophone. The ţambal is played by striking the instrument's metal strings, which are stretched from end to end, with two small hammers.

A gifted violinist, Romanian Georges Enesco is best known as the twentieth-century composer who preserved Romanian folk songs by incorporating them into his compositions. The two Romanian rhapsodies he composed are probably his best-loved works.

Above: In Romania, folk dances fall into one of two broad categories: ritual or entertainment. Ritualized dances are usually performed during religious ceremonies or special cultural occasions, such as harvest celebrations. The Fecioreasca, Hora, Purtata, Oltenasul, and Chindia are just some of Romania's many folk dances. Because the various dances date back to different periods in history, they also feature distinctly different dance steps and gestures, as well as different styles of music.

Handicrafts

Many Romanians earn a living by selling handicrafts made at home or in small village workshops. The handicrafts produced in each region vary according to the natural resources that are readily available. Famous Romanian handicrafts include wooden or stone carvings, pottery, handwoven carpets, and heavily ornamented, colorful costumes. Although both women and men produce handicrafts in Romania, the types of crafts made are gender specific. Carving and pottery, for example, are male-dominated crafts, while women tend to excel at sewing and weaving.

Embroidery is a skill for which Romanian women are admired. Often with little more than the most basic combination of needle and thread, rural Romanian women produce some of the finest and most intricate designs on pieces of fabric, usually tablecloths. Handmade Romanian folk costumes are brightly colored and heavily ornamented. The costumes often sell for high prices in Western countries because the sewing skill and the intensely laborious process behind the finished product is immediately apparent.

Below: **In Romania, many rural homes still contain hand-operated looms that the women of the household use to make rugs or carpets.**

Leisure and Festivals

Romanians are a traditionally hardworking people, but they also know how to have fun and enjoy themselves. In the summer, when some factories close for a month, many families go on long vacations to other parts of the country, such as the Black Sea's shore or the Carpathian Mountains. When at home, many Romanians enjoy chatting over a meal and bonding with family members. Romanians also love chess and card games, such as rummy.

Only the more affluent Romanians can afford to pay for entertainment on weekends. Some spend weekend afternoons playing tennis or golf, while others begin the evening with a meal at a favorite restaurant before watching a movie. Younger affluent Romanians favor going to dance clubs to meet new people and dance the night away.

Holidays in the Country

Some Romanians spend their summer vacations camping in the forests to experience nature or swimming and fishing in the country's river valleys. Barbecues are also popular during the summer, when family and friends gather for a meal and an evening spent in the open enjoying the good weather.

MINERAL WATER

Romania is home to many thermal and mineral springs. Waters from these springs contain different compositions of minerals and are believed by some to cure certain ailments. Some springs have been converted into commercially run spas, which attract thousands of local and foreign visitors each year.
(A Closer Look, page 62)

Left: **Two older Romanians in Braşov enjoy a leisurely game of chess — and each other's company.**

After the fall of communism in 1989, many rural Romanians, including farmers living in areas frequented by tourists, opened up boardinghouses on their homesteads. Offering relatively inexpensive lodging, these establishments are especially attractive to those living in the city and seeking a weekend getaway in the country. The promise of fresh air, relaxing natural surroundings, and traditional, home-cooked Romanian meals have turned these boardinghouses into profitable businesses.

Culture

The country's many museums sponsor a variety of arts and cultural festivals throughout the year. Frequent performances in Romania's theaters and opera houses also help satisfy those who are culturally inclined.

Every year, thousands of Romanians and tourists alike visit Sighişoara for the Medieval Art Festival, which is aimed at recreating the atmosphere of the medieval past. Theater groups stage performances from or related to medieval times, while musicians perform concerts. Individual artists and artisans also have exhibitions showcasing their medieval-inspired works. Sighişoara is an appropriate setting for the festival because it is one of Europe's best-preserved medieval towns.

NATURE AND EXTREME SPORTS

Romania's diverse natural landscapes are not only scenic; they are also ideal settings for enthusiasts of extreme sports. Many Romanians love visiting the mountains (*above*) for their breathtaking scenery and for the great number of sporting activities that can be pursued there. In summer, rock climbing, trekking, and mountain biking are popular activities, while skiing and sledding are enjoyed in winter. Romanians who favor diving often visit the Black Sea.

Sports

Romanians generally enjoy sports, and soccer is the national favorite. Romanians love playing soccer as much as they enjoy watching it, whether at home on the television or in a stadium supporting their favorite teams. The country's national soccer team became famous in the 1994 World Cup soccer championship, held in the United States. That year, the Romanian team reached the quarter-finals, in which they lost a match to Sweden. Through heated competition, Romania's various soccer clubs have maintained high standards for the sport within the country. In 1986, Steaua Bucharest won the European Cup. Gheorgh Hagi, Gica Popescu, Adrian Mutu, Adrian Ilie, and Cristian Chivu are some of Romania's more famous soccer players. Hagi, whose performance at the 1994 World Cup championship awed spectators and club managers, has since played for a number of prestigious soccer teams, such as Steaua Bucharest, Turkey's Galatasaray Istanbul, and Spain's Real Madrid. Today, many talented Romanian soccer players play for Italian, Spanish, English, and Dutch teams.

NADIA COMĂNECI

Nadia Comăneci made sporting history in the 1976 Olympics, held in Montreal, Canada. A talented gymnast, she became the first in the world to achieve a perfect score for her performance.
(A Closer Look, page 54)

Below: **In 1981, the Romanian national soccer team played England at Wembley Stadium in London.**

Left: **Born in Bucharest in 1946, Ilie Nastase gained worldwide fame in the early 1970s when he was ranked the world's number one player twice (1972 and 1973). He won the U.S. Open in 1972 and the French Open in 1973. Nastase went on to win more than one hundred professional titles, including fifty-seven singles titles, in the course of his illustrious tennis career.**

Soccer is only one of many sports enjoyed in Romania. Other popular pastimes include tennis, table tennis, running, hiking, cycling, skiing, kayaking, sailing, and swimming. The country has numerous sporting clubs and associations, many of which are supervised by the Ministry of Youth and Sports.

Sports Excellence

Romania has a strong history in athletic competition and ranked eleventh in the world for the number of medals won at the 2000 Olympic games held in Sydney, Australia. In 1984, however, Romania came in third in the medal count at the Olympic games held in Los Angeles — a remarkable feat for a relatively small country. Of the fifty-three medals Romanians took home, twenty were gold.

Gymnast Nadia Comăneci, tennis player Ilie Nastase, long-distance runner Gabriela Szabo, and kayaker Ivan Patzaichin are some of Romania's greatest sporting heros. In the 2000 Olympics, Romanians won gold medals in track and field, fencing, gymnastics, kayaking, rowing, and swimming. Diana Mocanu became the first Romanian swimmer in history to win an Olympic gold medal.

Left: A carnival on the streets of Bucharest draws as many delighted participants as curious bystanders.

CELEBRATING JUNII BRAŞOVULUI

Junii Braşovului, also known as the "Lads of Braşov," is a traditional festival celebrated in Braşov each spring. The celebration includes a lavish ceremonial procession, as well as much singing and dancing.
(A Closer Look, page 50)

Festivals of the Seasons

Romanians celebrate a host of religious and secular festivals every year. The country experiences four distinct seasons, and at least one major celebration marks each season. In spring, it is customary for a young Romanian man to give an amulet to the woman he loves. The amulet is made by knitting two tassels together: one red and one white. The white tassel signifies pureness, while the red tassel represents love. In Moldavia, this custom is not restricted to dating or newlywed couples; Romanians there give amulets to every person they cherish.

Celebrating the year's harvest, *Drăgaica* (DRAH-GUY-kaah) is a summer festival with a long history in Romania. The earliest reference to Drăgaica was recorded by Dimitrie Cantemir, a Moldavian noble, in the early eighteenth century. Drăgaica celebrations are most lavish in southern and southeastern Romania, where most of the country's agriculture is centered. The festival's main dance is performed by a group of young girls and a boy. During the performance, the girls gather in a circle to dance and sing along to a piper's accompaniment, while the boy hoists a pole with a figure of a person attached to the top. The figure has outstretched arms and is made of ears of corn.

SORCOVA

In winter, the Romanian custom of *Sorcova* (SOR-KOH-vaah) is celebrated on New Year's Eve. The sorcova, which is symbol of fertility, health, and purity, is a small bouquet children lightly brush over the heads of adults for good luck. In return for this gesture, children receive gifts of cakes, sweets, or money. Traditionally, children would gather twigs for their bouquets from several types of fruit trees, such as apple, pear, cherry, and plum, one month before the festival and care for them so they would bud by New Year's Eve. Today, most people use a twig from an apple or pear tree and symbolically decorate it with colored paper.

Easter Traditions

Easter celebrations in Romania involve special traditions that make the festival quite different from Easter celebrations elsewhere in the world. Easter egg painting, for example, although not unique to Romania, is taken to new heights in the country. Romanians use a *condei* (KON-day), which is a sharp, penlike instrument, to etch intricate, colored, designs onto the shells of hard-boiled eggs. Red, blue, green, and yellow are favorite traditional colors. The designs are mostly inspired by the country's folk culture, and popular designs include geometric patterns, stylized flowers, and cross or sun shapes.

Romanians also have a tradition of baking sweet breads or cakes for Easter and other religious festivals. For Easter, the breads often come in the shape of a knot, a cross, or a man, and they are supposed to represent the face and body of Christ. Romanian Easter breads come in a variety of flavors and fillings, which traditionally include cottage cheese, walnuts, and rice. Chocolate is sometimes used in more modern Easter breads.

Below: **Colorful Easter eggs decorated with intricate designs are a Romanian specialty.**

Food

Romanian food is rich and flavorful. One recipe often requires numerous ingredients, including a type of meat, various kinds of vegetables, and plenty of herbs and spices. Preparing Romanian dishes can be labor-intensive and time-consuming.

Romanians eat three main meals a day: breakfast, lunch, and dinner. A light breakfast is followed by lunch, which is considered the main meal of the day. Lunch always begins with a bowl of sour soup and some crusty bread. Soup is usually followed by a sizable serving of meat and potatoes or fish and salad. Most Romanians end lunch with desserts, which can range from puddings to cakes to fresh, seasonal fruit.

Romanian dinners are less filling and often consist of local favorites, such as stuffed peppers, meatballs, or grilled sausages. *Sarmale* (SAAR-mah-leh) is a favorite dish that was traditionally prepared only for Christmas. Sarmale is commonly called "cabbage rolls" because leaves of cabbage are used to wrap a stuffing that consists of minced meat, onions, rice, and various spices. The rolls are cooked first in a pan with tomato paste and then baked in an oven until they turn golden brown. Another

THE FIRST MEAL OF THE DAY

In Romania, breakfast usually consists of a warm drink, which can be coffee or tea for adults and milk for children, and some bread or toast. Some Romanians eat their morning bread with butter and jam, while others prefer the salty taste of cold cuts and cheese. Eggs, which may be cooked in a variety of ways, are also popular in the morning.

ROMANIAN WINES

Romania has a long tradition of wine making that dates back to the Romans. Since then, Romanian wine makers have been influenced by French methods, and wine drinkers in Romania have adopted some German and Austrian habits. Famous wine-producing regions include Tărnave, Dealu Mare, Murfatlar, and Cotnari. Tărnave is famous for white wines, while Dealu Mare is better known for red wines.

Left: Nearly every Romanian meal starts with a small glass of *tuică* (TSUI-ke), which is a fruit brandy typically made from plums.

Left: **A lunch of grilled pike or another type of fish is common for Romanians who live near the Danube River or the Black Sea.**

Romanian favorite is *mititei* (MEE-tee-tay), or grilled sausages. Recipes for mititei vary slightly from region to region, but the basic mixture typically consists of a combination of minced beef and mutton or pork, beef stock, crushed garlic, black pepper, and a choice of dried herbs.

A Love for Soups

Romanians have many recipes for soups. *Ciorba de potroace* (CHOWR-bah DE POH-trow-ah), or turkey soup, is made by boiling bony parts of a turkey in water with rice and chopped vegetables, such as carrots, celery, or onions. The soup is then flavored with salt, pepper, lemon juice, parsley, and dill. *Ciorba de burta* (CHOWR-bah DE BOORD-tah) is a soup made from tripe, which is the stomach tissue of a cow, sheep, or goat. The tripe and a small piece of fatty beef are first cut into tiny pieces and then boiled in water seasoned with salt, pepper, and a bay leaf. Chopped carrots and celery are then added and boiled until they become soft. When the soup is nearly ready, a mixture of egg yolks and vinegar is stirred in. Crushed garlic is sometimes added to give the soup a sharper flavor.

CORN PORRIDGE

In addition to bread and potatoes, Romanians also eat *mămăliguţă* (MAAH-maah-lee-GOOH-tsah), a thick corn porridge, as a staple food. The dish is relatively easy to prepare and consists of a boiled mixture of corn flour, salt, and water. *Balmush* (BAAL-mush) is another Romanian favorite. Served piping hot, balmush is essentially mămăliguţă with added butter and cheese.

A CLOSER LOOK AT ROMANIA

Romania is a country of astounding natural beauty and geographical diversity. In addition to the Carpathian Mountains in the country's interior, the Black Sea to the east, and the Danube River to the south, Romania is home to unique land formations known as the Muddy Volcanoes. The country also features numerous underground caves, which house an intriguing array of organisms adapted to living in total darkness.

Romanian culture is no less fascinating, with many age-old traditions and customs, such as the festival of Junii Braşovului, still celebrated today. Dracula, a fictional characer that has

Opposite and *below:* In keeping with tradition, many Romanians today still practice agriculture for a living.

captured the imaginations of millions, is based on the historical Romanian figure Vlad Ţepeş, better known as Vlad the Impaler.

Romanian arts and intellectualism soared in the period between World Wars I and II. Prominent Romanians of the time included playwright Eugène Ionesco, violinist and composer Georges Enesco, and philosopher Mircea Eliade.

In the 1980s, the dictator Nicolae Ceauşescu built the monumental House of the People, known today as the Palace of Parliament, in central Bucharest. Ceauşescu's regime left many parts of Romania environmentally damaged.

Bucharest

The capital of Romania, Bucharest boasts an eclectic mix of modern steel-and-glass buildings, boulevards and squares, historic churches, and communist buildings. Located in Walachia, Bucharest is the administrative, political, economic, and cultural center of the country.

According to Romanian legend, Bucharest was founded by a shepherd named Bucur. The first documented mention of the city was in 1459, when it was recorded as a residence of Vlad the Impaler, the ruler of Walachia. Bucharest served as the capital of Walachia between 1659 and 1862 and became the capital of Romania in 1862.

Bucharest's Modern History

After World War II and the rise of the Ceaușescu regime in 1965, Bucharest fell into a state of decline. In 1977, an earthquake shook the city, killing about 1,500 people and destroying many buildings. Following this disaster, dictator Nicolae Ceausescu introduced extensive rebuilding programs designed to remodel

Below: The Romanian Athenaeum is one of the grandest historical buildings still standing in Bucharest.

create a city center that reflected communist values. Heavy fighting during the revolution that ousted the Ceausescu regime in December 1989 caused damage to many of these buildings and prominent landmarks.

Above: **More than two million Romanians live in Bucharest, which is divided into six districts.**

A City of Attractions

Since 1989, Bucharest has seen rapid growth, and it is now a popular tourist destination. Favorite attractions include Biserica Curtea Veche (Old Court Church), Antim Monastery, and Stavropoleos and Spiridon churches; the Romanian Athenaeum; the open-air Village Museum; and the National Museum of Art. The Romanian Athenaeum, the city's most prestigious concert and exhibition hall, was built by French architect Albert Galleron in the 1880s. The Village Museum, which was established in 1936, displays village architecture and crafts from all over Romania. Founded in 1948, the National Museum of Art houses a large collection of Romanian and other European art.

Călușari

Dance of the Călușari

Romanian folk dances are colorful and lively. One of the most popular Romanian folk dances is the dance of the Călușari. This dance was traditionally performed by a group of men who belonged to a mystical religious group called the Călușari. To members of the group, the dance was a form of worship believed to have magical powers. In recent times, many Romanian folk dance troupes and musical associations have adapted the dance and made it popular.

Origins

The dance of the Călușari was originally believed to be a fertility rite, in which spirits were asked to bless married couples with many children. The dance was also performed to heal illnesses. Over time, the dance evolved into other ritual dances for different purposes, such as seeking divine help in fighting a war.

Traditional Călușari dancers, all men, were bound together by oath and had to stay with the group for a certain number of years. A nominated leader headed the group, which usually consisted of seven or nine dancers. The group of men lived by

Left: **Romanian folklore states that the Călușari had an ancient history and were blessed with magical powers, but nobody knows for certain when or how the traditions of the Călușari first started.**

the rules of the Căluşari. Rehearsals took place in secret, which only added to the air of mystery and magic surrounding the Căluşari. Today, it is uncertain how many Romanian men participate in the Căluşari.

Above: **Modern Romanians emphasize the cultural and entertainment value of the Căluşari dance value over its religious significance.**

Pomp and Ceremony

The Căluşari dance in modern times focuses on the actual dance steps and the colorful costumes. The dancers are lively and rhythmic as they dance around a pole and hit the ground with sticks or whips. The dancers also leap high over a masked dancer, who represents the buffoon, or clown, of the troupe. His role is to make the audience laugh. Sometimes young children are passed to the dancers during the during the performance in hopes the power of the dance will protect the children from illnesses.

The dance of the Căluşari has become an important part of modern Romania's folk-dance tradition. The dances are performed year-round in theaters, music halls, and village and town squares. Many dance troupes have reworked and adapted the dance with more modern interpretations.

Caves: The World Underground

Romania has some of the world's most extensive cave systems. Geologists, biologists, and other scientists have been studying these caves to discover how they were formed and what kind of life-forms are able to survive in total darkness. In Romania, the main organizations involved in the exploration of caves are the Romanian Speleological Institute, which is based both in Bucharest and in Cluj-Napoca, as well as the Romanian Speleological Federation, also based in Cluj-Napoca. Speleology is the scientific study and exploration of caves.

There are more than 12,000 caves in Romania. These caves consist of many different types. Romania's largest and most important caves are situated in the karst areas near the Southern Carpathians. These caves include the Cioclovina, Vantului, Polovraci, and Cornilor caves.

Movile Cave

Movile Cave is perhaps the most fascinating of Romania's caves. Discovered in 1986, Movile Cave is close to the Black Sea coast

ABOUT CAVES

Caves are natural openings in Earth. They are formed by different processes and in different types of rock. The most common type of cave is formed by the chemical reaction of groundwater and limestone. Limestone caves are usually part of what is called a karst landscape, which features rough exposed rock, sinkholes, and caves. The unusual karst terrain forms when bedrock is dissolved by water that drains away, leaving behind the large holes we call caves. Not all caves, however, are formed in this way. Glacier caves are formed by melting ice in glaciers, while sea caves are formed by the erosion of rock caused by wind and water currents. Volcanic caves are created by flowing lava and the effect of volcanic gases.

Left: **The Cioclovina cave is known to have a large deposit of phosphate.**

48

Left: The Ponorici cave is located in the western part of the Southern Carpathians.

and is the only example of a cave ecosystem supported entirely by chemosynthesis, which is the production of organic molecules using chemical rather than light energy. All the organisms found in Movile Cave can survive without light and would, in fact, be harmed if exposed to light.

Movile Cave's ecosystem has one of the largest numbers of species ever recorded in a cave. More than thirty of these species were previously unknown and exist nowhere else in the world. These species include many types of millipedes, scorpions, spiders, and worms. These creatures have adapted to their dark environment by learning to navigate without sight. They survive on bacteria and fungi that absorb energy from the sulfurous hot springs found beneath the cave.

The unique composition of the air and water in Movile Cave is the key to its amazing ecology. The water contains high levels of hydrogen sulfide, while the air is rich in carbon dioxide and methane, but lacks oxygen. The chemical composition of the water and air in the cave is unlike that in any cave previously discovered. For this reason, conservation efforts have been aimed at preventing external light, air, and water from entering the cave. Ordinary water and air would destroy the fragile ecosystem in this wonderfully rich underground world.

Below: The Sura Mare cave is also located in the western part of the Southern Carpathians and is relatively easy to reach and explore.

Celebrating Junii Braşovului

Every spring, near the time of the Romanian Orthodox Easter, residents of the Schei district of the city of Braşov celebrate a traditional festival called Junii Braşovului, or the "Lads of Braşov." The main attraction of Junii Braşovului celebrations is the procession of men dressed in traditional costumes and riding horses through the old streets of Braşov.

Origins of the Festival

The exact origins of Junii Braşovului are unknown, but the festival began during the period in Romanian history when Transylvania was successively dominated by various foreign powers, including the Ottoman Turks, the Austrians, and the Hungarians. The festival was meant to preserve age-old customs and promote nationalistic values. Historically, the procession was spread over five days, starting on Monday. Each day, the men would ride to a different location, where an important event, such as a significant turning point in history or the death

Left: **Churches and other medieval buildings give Braşov, located in central Romania, a special charm.**

of a hero, had taken place. On the first day, for example, the procession could begin at the site where Craisorul, a local hero, was buried.

The Seven Groups of Junii

Today, the Junii Braşovului procession is divided into seven main groups: the Young Junii, the Old Junii, the Whitish Junii, the Turkey Junii, the Horseman Junii, the Dorobanti Junii, and the Junii of the Old City. Each group has a specific flag and a unique colorful costume. Even the horses are decorated according to the groups to which they belong.

For the modern viewer, the procession is a treat for the senses. A combination of colorful festivities, rich traditions, and historical significance, the procession culminates in a lively celebration that includes singing, dancing, and feasting. Members of the Young Junii also continue the tradition of participating in a mace-throwing competition. A mace is similar to a staff or baton.

Cleaner Living

Heavy and rapid industrialization during the communist and Ceaușescu years caused some parts of Romania to become extremely polluted, a condition the postcommunist government is still trying to correct today.

Environmental Horrors

Formerly nicknamed the "Black City," Copsa Mica had probably the country's worst example of air pollution when communism came to an end in 1989. For decades, two factories — one producing tires and the other metal products — spewed pollutants out of their chimneys every day. Romanians who worked in the factories and whose families lived in the surrounding areas bore the brunt of the pollution's adverse effects. Health experts reported that as many as half of the city's inhabitants suffered from bronchitis or asthma and that many of the children suffered varying degrees of mental retardation.

In 2000, two industrial accidents devastated the Danube River system. First, a gold mine in Baia Mare leaked lethal amounts of cyanide into nearby streams that flow into the Tisza

Left: Previously, Copsa Mica was so polluted that plants could not grow. The fumes from the factories carried black dust particles that covered every exposed surface, including people's faces. Today, since the clean-up operation in the early 1990s, Romanians in the region are again cultivating gardens.

River, a major tributary of the Danube. Most of the fish and plants supported by the Tisza perished, and people in Romania, Hungary, and the former Yugoslavia were badly affected. Second, the dam of a mining operation's wastewater resevoir gave way under the combined pressure of heavy rain and melting snow and leaked tons of toxic zinc and lead into a tributary of the Tisza. The mine is located in Baia Borsa, a small town near Baia Mare.

Government Action

Since 1989, the Romanian government has been working hard to reverse the legacy of communist industrialization. In 1990, the Ministry of Environment, which was renamed the Ministry of Waters, Forests, and Environment Protection in 1992, was established. The ministry supervises more than forty local agencies, including the Danube Delta Biosphere Reserve Administration, which closely monitor the environment and enforce laws and regulations that protect the environment in their respective regions. Through the work of the ministry, the Romanian government hopes to meet the requirements to become a European Union (EU) member. In 2001, an EU report stated that Romania has made significant progress, although improved funding, more effective agencies, and more efficient ways of implementing plans were still needed.

Opposite: Since the fall of communism, scenes of dark smoke rising from industrial smokestacks, such as this one at a steel factory in Galaţi, are increasingly becoming a thing of the past.

Nadia Comăneci

A dedicated and talented athlete, Nadia Comăneci first captivted the world with her gymnastic feats at the 1976 Olympic Games in Montreal. She dominated women's gymnastic events during the Olympics and did much to popularize the sport among the general public.

The Girl Who Changed the Olympics

Born in 1961 in Oneşti, Nadia Comăneci caught the attention of renowned gymnastics coach Bèla Karolyi, who later became the Romanian gymnastics coach, when she was only six years old. She soon joined the Romanian junior gymnastics team and competed in her first national junior championship event in 1969. She won the championship the following year. Continuing to win all-around titles in her age group, Comăneci competed in her first senior competition in 1975, when she entered the European Championship. She caused a stir in the gymnastics world when she beat Russia's five-time European champion Lyudmilla Turishcheva, winning four gold medals and one silver.

In 1976, fourteen-year-old Comăneci traveled to Canada as a member of the Romanian national gymnastics team to compete in the Olympic Games. She awed spectators and judges with her routines, winning gold medals in the uneven bars, balance beam, and all-around events; a silver medal in the team competition; and a bronze medal for the floor exercises event. Her medal tally, however, is not the only achievement for which she is remembered. Comăneci became the first gymnast in Olympic history to receive a perfect ten score, which she was awarded for the uneven bars event in the team competition. She went on to score six more perfect tens during the competition.

Further Successes

Comăneci successfully defended her European Championship all-around title in the following two competitions. In the 1980 Olympic Games in Moscow, she won two gold medals for the balance beam and floor exercise events and silver medals for the all-around and team events. In 1984, Comăneci retired from amateur gymnastics.

Above: **For her achievements at the 1976 Olympic Games, Comăneci became the youngest Romanian to be awarded the Hero of Socialist Labor medal.**

AN INSPIRATION TO OTHERS

Comăneci's success has spurred many young Romanian girls to follow in her footsteps. Competition is tough, however, and very few aspiring gymnasts make the country's national gymnastics team.

Opposite: **When Comăneci scored her first perfect ten at the Montreal Olympic Games in 1976, the scoreboard showed 1.00 because the computerized scoring system had not been programmed to register the number ten.**

Dracula

Romania has long been associated with the Transylvanian vampire Count Dracula, the fictional character created by Bram Stoker in his 1897 novel *Dracula*. The book is regarded as a masterpiece of Gothic horror fiction, and many people believe Stoker based his notorious character on the colorful life of Vlad Ţepeş, who ruled the principality of Walachia in the 1400s.

More Than a Myth

Born in about 1431, Vlad Ţepeş became prince of Walachia when Vlad Dracul, his father and ruler of the principality, was murdered in 1448. Vlad Ţepeş ruled for only two months before he was forced into exile and replaced by Vladislav II. He reclaimed his throne in 1456 and ruled for the next six years.

Vlad was a strong ruler who fiercely defended his people and principality. He forged renewed resistance against the Ottoman Turks, who had demanded payment of heavy taxes since 1391, and fought off Hungarian efforts to restore its domination over the area.

Vlad was regarded as an upholder of law and order. He quickly developed a reputation of ruthlessness, as he quashed any opposition to his rule with an iron fist. He impaled thousands

WHAT THE NAME MEANS

Vlad Ţepeş's father, Vlad Dracul, belonged to the Order of the Dragon, an organization that was dedicated to fighting the Ottoman Turks. Because the symbol of the order was a dragon, he took on the name *Dracul* (DRAH-cool). Dracul means "dragon" or "devil" in Romanian. Vlad Ţepeş inherited the title after his father's death, and he adopted the name Dracula, meaning "son of the dragon."

Left: **Often referred to as Dracula's Castle, Bran Castle is located in the village of Bran, which is southwest of Braşov. The castle was built in 1377 to protect the city from invaders.**

BRAM STOKER'S DRACULA

Since the publication of Bram Stoker's *Dracula* in 1897, many people have come to regard Count Dracula and Vlad the Impaler as one and the same person. The factual similarities between Count Dracula and Vlad, however, are limited. Although Stoker borrowed the name Dracula and a few facts from Walachian history, the rest of the novel is pure fiction.

Since the book's publication, ideas of Count Dracula and vampirism have been interpreted and represented in many ways. Over a thousand books have been written on the subject, and dozens of movies have been made, the most famous of which include *Nosferatu* (1929), *Dracula* (1931), *Bram Stoker's Dracula* (1992), and *Interview with the Vampire* (1994).

of people whom he regarded as traitors, would-be traitors, or enemies of Walachia. His brutal punishments deterred crime in the principality and struck fear in the hearts of his enemies. By the time of his death, he had killed an estimated 40,000 to 100,000 people. As a result, many Romanians came to call him Vlad Ţepeş, which translates as "Vlad the Impaler."

In 1462, Vlad was arrested and imprisoned by Hungarian king Matthias Corvinus. He was eventually released and briefly ruled Walachia again in 1476 before being killed in battle at the end of that same year. How Vlad died or who killed him is shrouded in mystery. Legends say he was either killed by a Turkish assassin or was mistaken for a Turk on the battlefield and accidentally killed by his own men.

A Romanian Hero

Today, many Romanians regard Vlad the Impaler as a national hero. Despite his cruelties and severe punishments, Romanians are proud of his military successes against the Ottoman Turks in fighting to retain Walachia's independence. He is honored in songs and folktales, most notably in the villages that surround his castle in the northern part of the Walachian region.

House of the People

Ceauşescu — A Megalomaniac

Nicolae Ceauşescu (1918-1989) came to power in 1965 and, in less than twenty years, turned Romania into a starving police state. With the help of his family members, whom he appointed to fill key governmental positions, and the Securitate (Secret Police), Ceauşescu did nearly anything he wanted. Probably the most monumental of his schemes was the building of the Boulevard of Socialist Victory in central Bucharest. Beginning in 1984, as much as one-third of old, historical Bucharest was bulldozed in pursuit of Ceauşescu's grand plans and lopsided vision. Inspired by his visit to North Korea thirteen years earlier, Ceauşescu wanted to match, if not outdo, the grandeur of the new political and architectural center he saw in North Korea's capital city, Pyongyang.

The Highlight of the Boulevard

At the center of Ceauşescu's costly architectural vision was the gargantuan structure he named the House of the People, or Casa Poporului. Ironically, Ceauşescu never got to enjoy what he built;

Below: The massive construction project for the House of the People consumed badly needed funds, causing extreme poverty and senseless suffering. As a result, many Romanians called for the House of the People to be blown up after the Ceauşescus were executed. The requests were dismissed, however, because the sheer amount of explosives needed was too costly for the impoverished Romanian economy to bear.

he was overthrown and executed shortly after the building was completed. Today, the structure is known as the Palace of Parliament and houses the Romanian parliament. Most of the building remains unused.

The Palace of Parliament rises twelve stories, or about 276 feet (84 m) high; has more than 3,000 rooms; and has a surface area of about 395,000 square yards (330,000 sq m). The largest room, Sala Unirii, which means "Unification Hall," has a ceiling that slides. Originally intended as a precautionary measure, the ceiling, when open, is wide enough to allow a helicopter to land in and take off from the hall, in the event such action is necessary.

The building contains numerous grand staircases and marbled halls, some 3,500 tons (3,175 metric tons) of crystal in the form of chandeliers, and a carpet so large it had to be woven on the premises with specially designed machines. The finished carpet in Unification Hall reportedly weighs fourteen tons (12.7 metric tons). The largest chandelier in the building weighs approximately three tons (2.7 metric tons) and uses seven thousand bulbs.

Above: **To make way for the Boulevard of Socialist Victory in Bucharest, many historical buildings were demolished. The razed buildings included old homes, churches, monasteries, and synagogues that once stood in the districts of Rahova, Antim, and Uranus.**

Intellectual Life, Art, and Culture

Romanian culture and intellectualism flourished during the period between World War I and World War II. From artists to academics, many Romanians of the time became important figures of the twentieth century.

Constantin Brancuşi (1876–1957)

Born in Hobitza, Romanian sculptor Constantin Brancuşi is considered a pioneer of modern abstract sculpture. He is known for his abstract sculpture of egg-shaped heads and birds in flight. Brancusi used many materials for his sculptures, including marble, bronze, and wood. Some of his best-known works include *The Kiss* (1908), *Maiastra* (1912), *Beginning of the World* (1924), and *Torso of a Young Girl* (1922).

Eugène Ionesco (1909–1994)

One of the most famous playwrights of the twentieth century, Eugène Ionesco was born in Slatina, Romania. He eventually settled in Paris in 1945 and began writing plays. *The Bald Soprano*

TRISTAN TZARA (1896–1963)

Romanian-born poet Tristan Tzara is mainly known as the founder of Dada, an artistic movement of the early 1900s that advocated the destruction of all values of civilized society. In *Seven Dada Manifestos* (1924), Tzara explained the philosophy of the Dada movement. He is also credited with writing the first Dada texts: *The First Heavenly Adventure of Mr. Antipyrine* (1916) and *Twenty-Five Poems* (1918). Tzara eventually grew disillusioned with the Dada movement and began writing more accessible poetry.

Left: In Romania, Brancuşi's public sculptures can be found in Tîrgu Jiu, where he first received formal training in carving. These enormous steel works are entitled *Endless Column, Gate of the Kiss,* and *Table of Silence.* Today, Brancuşi's works are featured in museums and private collections worldwide, as well as in galleries in Romania.

(1949) created a revolution in dramatic techniques and helped establish the Theater of the Absurd, a theatrical movement that portrays human life as absurd and lacking purpose. Absurdist plays often feature characters in bizarre situations. A scene from *The Bald Soprano*, for example, features conversations between two seeming strangers who later discover they are actually husband and wife. Ionesco wrote many more plays, including *The Lesson* (1951), *The Chairs* (1952), *The New Tenant* (1955), and *Rhinoceros* (1959).

Mircea Eliade (1907–1986)

Born in Bucharest, Mircea Eliade is a famous philosopher and historian. He studied philosophy at the University of Bucharest before going to Calcutta, India to study Indian philosophy and Sanskrit. While in India, he began formulating his ideas on the relationship between language, symbolism, religious traditions, and mystical experiences. On his return to Romania, he earned a doctorate in 1933 at the University of Bucharest, where he began teaching. In 1945, Eliade accepted a teaching post at the Sorbonne University in Paris. Thirteen years later, he became a professor of religious studies at the University of Chicago in the United States, where he remained until his death.

ELIADE'S WORKS

The modern academic study of the history and philosophy of religion owes a great debt to the writings and ideas of Mircea Eliade. Eliade's most famous writings include *Patterns of Comparative Religion* (1949) and *Shamanism: Archaic Techniques of Ecstasy* (1951). Eliade also compiled a three-volume work entitled *A History of Religious Ideas* (1985) that took him eight years to complete. In addition, he was editor-in-chief of the sixteen-volume *Encyclopedia of Religion* (1987) and founded the journal *History of Religions* in 1961.

Mineral Water

Romania has about three thousand mineral and thermal springs, about one-third of Europe's total. Although these springs are located throughout the country, most can be found along the Carpathian Mountains.

Bottled in Romania

The springs are a natural feature of Romania's landscape and are also crucial to the country's inhabitants and economy. Many villagers drink only mineral water because their homes are located near one of these natural springs. With the ever-increasing global demand for mineral water, the Romanian mineral water industry has grown significantly in recent years. Today, the country has a number of companies that specialize in producing bottled mineral water, some of it naturally sparkling. Dorna — Romania's leading brand of naturally sparkling mineral water — is now distributed to twenty-six European countries. Other well-known Romanian brands of mineral water are Borsec, Bucovina, and Harghita.

Below: **Natural springs such as the one shown here are commonly found in Romania.**

THE SPA OF HERCULES

Founded by the Romans, Băile Herculane (*left*) is the oldest and one of the most reputable spas in Romania. The spa is located in the southwestern part of the country. According to Roman legend, Băile Herculane is named after Hercules, the Greek mythological figure who is said to have cured the wounds inflicted by the Hydra — a nine-headed monster — by bathing in the mineral springs.

Romania's Favorite Spas

Romania is home to seventy health spas, all of which are valued for their medical properties. The spas' thermal waters and mineral-rich muds offer natural therapeutic treatments for various conditions, including rheumatic, neurological, digestive, and cardiovascular ailments.

Just outside the city of Oradea, Baile Felix is the country's largest spa. Due to the area's mild winters and moderate summers, it is particularly popular among people wishing to relieve rheumatic, inflammatory, and neurological ailments.

The spring waters from the Calimăneşti region were popular with French emperor Napoleon III, who had the waters exported to France for his personal consumption. Famous for its reputed curative properties, the spa's waters are believed to ease digestive and kidney problems, among other ailments.

A popular resort among women, Sovata is well-known for its saline waters that come from a nearby lake. The water becomes warmer and saltier toward the lake bed, while the bottom of the lake is lined with mineral-rich mud.

Muddy Volcanoes

The Muddy Volcanoes, as they are popularly known, are a unique geological feature found in the Eastern Carpathians of central Romania. This area lies close to the intersection of tectonic plates. Tectonic plates are large masses of land that float on Earth's mantle and continually move against each other, causing earthquakes, faults, and folds in Earth's crust. The Muddy Volcanoes are a result of this geological activity.

A Unique Landscape

The Muddy Volcanoes are located north of the city of Buzău, near the city of Berca, in an area with little vegetation. The hills and slopes are covered with cones that overflow with mud, causing the locals to call these formations "muddy volcanoes." The cones of the craters look like small volcanoes, while the mud that streams outs resembles volcanic lava. The crater cones are 16 to 20 feet (5 to 6 m) tall and are quite colorful. A white crust of crystallized salt rings each cone. Yellow and orange-red streaks of sulfur can be seen in the mud, which is colored in various shades

Left: The landscapes surrounding the Muddy Volcanoes often resemble honeycombs or gnarled tree bark.

ranging from light brown to black. The mud in the crater cones bubbles and releases a flammable gas called methane. As the mud overflows the craters, it moves slowly down the sides of the crater and begins to dry. At the bases of the cones, the dried mud creates shapes resembling honeycombs or the gnarled bark of old trees. Sometimes the cones are less prominent and the mud bubbles out from geysers and mud pools. Most plants cannot grow in this highly saline environment. However, some hardy plants, such as the gardurarita, have evolved to survive in the salty conditions.

Emerging from the Deep

The same processes that create ordinary volcanoes also created the Muddy Volcanoes. While magma in ordinary volcanoes emerges from deep within Earth, the gases that escape from the Muddy Volcanoes originate in a layer that does not reach as deep into Earth's crust. These gases, mostly methane, slowly build up and are released when there is movement in the tectonic plates, such as during an earthquake. The gases then rise through openings in Earth's crust and mix with a layer of underground water, creating the bubbling mud that can be seen oozing out of the Muddy Volcanoes.

OTHER INTERESTING GEOLOGICAL FEATURES

The Eastern Carpathians are also home to other interesting geological formations. At Andreiasu, near Focsani, there is a constant emission of natural gas that is called "The Unextinguished Fires." Under the Eastern Capathians are networks of huge faults and rifts, some running many hundreds of miles (km). These faults and rifts, such as the fault near Bisoca, separating the peaks and hills of the Eastern Carpathians, sometimes appear on the surface as well. They are most clearly seen from the air, as long gouges in the land.

People Power: The Revolution of 1989

How It All Started

On December 15, 1989, a small group of protestors gathered outside the home of Laszlo Tokes, an ethnic Hungarian pastor, in Timişoara. They were calling for the reinstatement of Tokes, who had been removed from his position because he criticized Ceauşescu's regime during his church services. By December 17, the minor protest had grown into an uprising in the city's Freedom Square. The Securitate and the army first drove tanks and armored cars into the square to disperse the crowds and later opened fire on the crowd, a move that Ceauşescu personally ordered. An uncertain but significant number of people were killed, and mass protests mushroomed in cities throughout the country, including Bucharest, Cluj-Napoca, and Sibiu.

Ceauşescu's Last Days

Ceauşescu, who had been in Iran on an official visit during the unrest, returned to Romania late on December 20. The next day,

Left: **All the Romanians buried in this Bucharest cemetery died during the 1989 revolution.**

Above: **Piata Libertatii, or Freedom Square, in Timişoara was where Romanians first clashed with communist authorities in 1989.**

he decided that he would manufacture an appearance of support for his government that would be broadcast live by both local and international media. The event went wrong for Ceauşescu. Noisy dissidents interrupted his speech, and many fearful audience members fled from what they believed would turn into a violent scene.

Despite riot-police action and numerous arrests, disenchanted Romanians remained in the city center, and more and more Romanians gradually took to the streets. By December 22, the revolution had gathered full force. Even the soldiers who had been sent to disperse the rioters turned their tanks and armored cars around and joined in the people's march toward the Communist Party's headquarters. The Ceauseşcus tried to escape by helicopter but were soon seized.

The End of an Era

On December 25, Nicolae Ceauşescu and his wife, Elena, were hastily tried in a military court. They were found guilty of causing the deaths of some 60,000 Romanians by ordering soldiers to fire into the crowds during the recent period of social unrest when army generals had refused to give the command. The Ceauşescus were executed by a firing squad immediately after the trial.

The Roma

The Roma are a distinct ethnic group. In the past, the Roma were called Gypsies, but this name is not preferred today. The number of Roma worldwide has been estimated at between 2 and 5 million. In Romania, the Roma number over 500,000. Some believe the number might be higher because many Roma are thought to have declared their ethnicity as Romanian or Hungarian. Officially, Romania has the largest population of Roma in Europe.

Lifestyle and Customs

The Roma were traditionally a nomadic people who moved from place to place in groups related by family or occupation. They took up jobs that enabled them to travel, such as animal herding, metalworking, and entertaining. The Roma set up camps at the edges of Romanian towns and villages. Today, however, more and more Roma have become settled.

Roma families tend to be large, with as many as eight children. There are many groups and clans within the Roma community. Each group is headed by a *bulibasa* (boo-lee-bah-

ORIGINS AND MIGRATIONS

Experts generally agree that the Roma arrived in Europe from northern India and are ethnically and linguistically linked to Indians. Roma immigration from northern India took place in stages. By the 1000s, the Roma had arrived in Persia. They were in southeastern Europe by the beginning of the 1300s, and in western Europe by the 1400s. From the 1950s onward, the Roma could be found on every inhabited continent.

Below: Few Romanian Roma today continue to lead a nomadic lifestyle.

SHAA), or chief, as well as by a judge, called a *stabor* (staa-BORH), who helps to settle disputes. Many Roma are Orthodox Christians, while a minority are Protestants or Roman Catholics. Most Roma communities are extremely poor, with little access to running water, electricity, health care, and education. Unemployment is high among young Roma men.

Into the Twenty-First Century

The Romanian government initiated a program to better integrate Roma into Romanian society. Roma children, for example, are now allowed to study Romany, the Roma language, in school. Young Roma have reserved places at universities, while older Roma are encouraged to attend literacy classes to learn how to read and write.

The Roma community has also obtained political representation in the Romanian government. A special unit within the Department of Interethnic Relations, the National Office for Roma, was set up in 2000 to support and coordinate development programs for the Roma community. Despite the postcommunist government's recent actions, many challenges remain for Romanian Roma. At the most basic level, the Roma continue to face discrimination from other Romanians and are often the victims of violent racist hate crimes.

TARAF DE HAIDOUKS

Taraf de Haidouks is the name of a Roma folk music group from Clejani that has gained international acclaim for their music. Their leader Nicolae Neascu, who died in 2002, gained fame as the most celebrated Roma violinist in the world. Taraf de Haidouks plays traditional Roma music and has performed in the United States. Their albums include *Evil Eye* (1994) and *Dumbala Dumba* (1998).

Sarmizegetusa: Ancient Ruins

Romania's ancient past is evident in the many Dacian and Roman ruins that can be found in parts of the country. Some of the most impressive Dacian ruins can be found in Sarmizegetusa in the Southern Carpathians, located in Hunedoara county. Other Dacian ruins can be found in Roşia Montană in Alba county.

The Dacians
In the first century B.C., the Romans advanced into the Balkan Peninsula and disrupted Dacian life. The Dacians were mainly an agricultural people. Led by Burebista, who ruled from 82 to 44 B.C., the various Dacian tribes united to resist the Roman intruders. When the Dacians grew into a rich and mighty state, they again attracted Roman interest. Between A.D. 101 and 106, the Roman emperor Trajan launched two attacks and seized the Dacian kingdom, including Sarmizegetusa, its capital.

A Complex System of Defenses
The Dacians are known for the complex system of defenses they constructed between 100 B.C. and A.D. 100. Built from a variety of materials, including stone and wood, this defense system

A PROTECTED HERITAGE

Preserving the ruins at Sarmizegetusa (*left*) and other Dacian historical sites is a challenge. Romania has few laws to protect these sites, which often fall victim to looters who dig illegally and remove artifacts from the ground. Some help from the international community came in 1999, when the United Nations Educational, Scientific, and Cultural Organization (UNESCO) placed six of Romania's Dacian fortresses on the World Heritage List. This means that UNESCO funds can be used to help preserve these ruins.

included fortified settlements and fortresses, many of which still exist as ruins today. The fortresses of Costesti-Cetatuie, Vărful lui Hulpe, and Sarmizegetusa protected roads leading to the Dacian cities and formed rings around them, while the fortresses of Costesti-Blidaru and Luncani-Piatra Rosie were built away from cities for strategic purposes.

Above: **Apart from the various fortresses, the Dacians also built a defense wall at Cioclovina-Ponorici. Built from wood and roughly hewn stones, this 1.6-mile (2.5-km)-long wall also had a series of perpendicular inner walls for added protection and security.**

An Ancient Temple

The most impressive ruins are at Sarmizegetusa, which was not only the political and military center of the Dacian kingdom, but also its religious center. The civil, military, and residential buildings of the city were rectangular or polygonal in shape, while the sacred spaces of the city were designed in circular shapes. The most important sacred ruins in of the city are those of Sarmizegetusa Regia, a large circular temple. The ruins of this temple consist of a horseshoe-shaped wooden structure surrounded by a stone circle. The design of the temple's pillars indicates that they served as a shadow clock and calendar, marking not only the passage of the sun across the sky, but also the passing of days, weeks, and months during the year.

Saving Ceauşescu's Child Victims

The plight of Romania's orphans came to light in the early 1990s, when the international media widely documented the atrocious conditions in which large numbers of orphans lived. Although much has been done since to try to correct the problem, child welfare is still a pressing social issue in Romania. As of 2002, about 43,000 children lived in institutions throughout the country.

Life in the Orphanages

During Ceauşescu's regime, approximately 100,000 Romanian children — sometimes called "Ceausescu's children" — lived in appalling conditions in large dormitory-style buildings run by the state. Due to lack of funding, the children were malnourished, inadequately clothed, and without access to education or basic medical care. Since 1989, steps have been taken to improve the living conditions within the country's orphanages and other institutions. Large orphanages are slowly being closed and replaced with facilities that accommodate smaller numbers of

Left: An estimated 2,000 children, mostly from orphanages or similar institutions, currently live on the streets of Romania, and about half can be found in Bucharest. Sleeping in shop doorways, sewers, or railway stations, many of these children resort to stealing or scavenging as a means to survive.

children, thus improving the ratio of staff to children. Unlike the Ceaușescu era, when children were left alone for hours on end, orphaned children today attend lessons and spend much of their time playing.

Above: **The children at this U.S.-assisted orphanage in Beiuş, Bihor county, are attending Bible class.**

A Brighter Future?

In June 2001, the Romanian government temporarily suspended international adoptions, which many felt encouraged families to abandon their babies. The following year, the government introduced a plan that supplemented the incomes of families most at risk of abandoning their children. Acknowledging the need to move away from the nation's widely criticized system of institutional care, the government also set the goal of halving the number of children in old-style institutions by the end of 2004 and housing them in more supportive surroundings. In addition, the Strategy for Protection of Children's Rights aims to reduce the number of children living in institutions by encouraging foster care and adoption within Romania. The problem, however, is far from being solved. Pediatric hospitals are still full of children abandoned after birth by their mothers because the mothers lack the basic necessities required to care for them.

RELATIONS WITH NORTH AMERICA

Although Romania and the United States officially established diplomatic relations in the late nineteenth century, interaction between the two nations was not significant for the most part until the early 1990s. It was not until World War I, when Romania fought against Germany, that ties between the two countries considerably strengthened. In the period between the two world wars, many U.S. investors opened factories in Romania. By the time World War II began, however, relations between Romania and the United States had become strained because Romania entered the war on the side of Germany. On August 23, 1944,

Opposite: **These women at a Romanian flag factory are making American flags that will be used in the celebratory events welcoming President George W. Bush to their country for the first time in 2002.**

Romania switched sides and became part of the Allied forces. The two nations officially reestablished diplomatic relations on February 7, 1946. In practice, however, the two nations were distanced until the early 1960s, when an agreement was reached to partially settle U.S. property claims in Romania.

Historically, relations between Romania and Canada have been limited and only official since the late 1960s. Following the fall of communism in 1989, however, the two nations have worked hard to build stronger trade and diplomatic ties. Today, Romania receives significant support from Canada.

Above: **U.S. president George W. Bush (*left*) and Romanian president Ion Iliescu (*right*) wave to a Romanian crowd before proceeding to a meeting discussing ties between their countries.**

Ties with the United States

Despite fundamental differences in political and governing systems, U.S. and Romanian leaders made frequent contact throughout the 1970s. In 1978, the Ceauşescus paid an official visit to the United States and were hosted in Washington, D.C. Earlier, in April 1975, a trade agreement was signed granting Romania the status of Most Favored Nation (MFN). Every year following, Romania's MFN status was reviewed by the U.S. Congress and renewed based on whether Romania's policies toward freedom of emigration were acceptable to the United States. By the mid-1980s, however, reports of violations in Romania of the human rights of religious and ethnic minorities prompted Congress to consider revoking Romania's MFN status on several occasions. In 1988, to preempt U.S. rejection, President Ceauşescu renounced MFN treatment from the United States.

In 1984, Romania was the only country in the Warsaw Pact that sent representatives to the Olympic Games held in Los Angeles. The decision was significant because the Soviet Union had boycotted the Olympic Games that year. Romania's participation was generally applauded by Americans, who

Below: **In August 1969, U.S. president Richard Nixon paid an official visit to Romania. His visit came after President Nicolae Ceauşescu had cleverly manipulated a position of Romanian independence that included befriending Israel and generally rejecting Soviet foreign policy.**

interpreted the act as a bold demonstration of independence from, if not defiance against, Moscow.

Since the fall of communism in 1989, the Romanian government has focused on adopting Western values and methods. In 1993, the U.S. Congress, suitably impressed by Romania's progress, restored the country's MFN status. By 1996, Romania was made a permanent recipient of MFN treatment. In 1997, U.S. president Bill Clinton visited Bucharest and introduced a partnership plan between the two countries. The plan sought to strengthen ties by encouraging mutual cooperation in pursuit of shared goals, including political and economic growth and regional security. In return, Romania has been supportive of the United States in the United Nations and also on other matters on the world stage. After September 11, 2001, when multiple terrorist attacks struck the United States, Romania has been openly supportive of the U.S.-led anti-terrorism campaign. In 2002, President George W. Bush paid an official visit to Bucharest to praise Romanians on their visible commitment to building a democracy and a free-market economy. That same year, Romania was welcomed into the North Atlantic Treaty Organization (NATO).

Ties with Canada

Romania and Canada established diplomatic relations on April 3, 1967. In 1976, Canada appointed its first ambassador to Romania, who was based at the Canadian embassy located in Bucharest. Romania set up its embassy in Ottawa in 1970. Romania also has consulate offices in Toronto and Montreal.

Today, political dialogue and trade talks dominate relations between Romania and Canada. Former Romanian president Emil Constantinescu was especially interested in building stronger Romanian-Canadian ties. Constantinescu was Romania's second democratically elected president, serving from 1996 to 2000, between President Ion Iliescu's first and second terms. Officials of the two countries each have only visited the other once. Constantinescu went to Canada in May 1998, and Canadian prime minister Jean Chrétien visited Romania in April 1996. The leaders and high-ranking diplomats of both countries, however, have met on numerous other occasions, including the 1997 NATO Summit held in Madrid and the 1999 summit for the Organization for Security and Cooperation in Europe (OSCE) held in Istanbul. At such meetings, representatives of both countries have often met with one another and reached mutually beneficial agreements relating to energy and telecommunications, among other important interests.

Left: **Romanian president Emil Constantinescu (*left*) and the premier of Quebec, Lucien Bouchard (*right*), pose for a photograph during the 1999 Francophone Summit held in Canada.**

The building of the first phase of Romania's nuclear power plant in Cernavodă became one of the key facilitators of current Romanian-Canadian ties. Canadian experts on atomic energy supervised the building of the nuclear project, which the Romanian government has promised the Canadian government will only be utilized for peaceful purposes. The first phase of the Cernavodă nuclear plant opened in 1996. Representatives from both Canada and Romania have since expressed interest in launching the construction of the plant's second phase.

Apart from trade, Canada's foreign policy toward Romania also includes promoting mutual support in matters of defense and the environment. Between the mid-1990s and the early 2000s, Romanian and Canadian ministers for defense, industry, the environment, and foreign affairs have carried out official visits to their counterparts' country in a bid to strengthen ties relating to their respective areas. Today, for example, it is not unusual for the armed forces of both countries to conduct joint training exercises. In Romania, these exercises usually take place in the Black Sea or the Carpathian Mountains.

Above: **Camella Macoviciuc (*left*) and Constanta Burcica (*right*) celebrate after winning the gold medal for the Women's Lightweight Double Scull event at the 1999 FISA Rowing Championships held in St. Catharines, Ontario.**

Trade Relations with the United States

Up until 1988, when President Ceauşescu renounced MFN treatment, Romania was the United States's largest trading partner in Eastern Europe. After 1988, however, Romanian products were heavily taxed in the United States and became unattractive to U.S. buyers. Trade relations improved significantly after November 1993, when the U.S. congress restored MFN status to Romania. Most Romanian goods became duty-free in the United States by February 1994 as a result. Romania's main exports to the United States include steel, machinery, and consumer goods, such as shoes and clothing. Romania's main imports from the United States are aircraft, electrical equipment, and food. In 2001, Romania purchased U.S. $375 million worth of U.S. goods and sold U.S. $520 million worth of exports to the United States. As of April 2002, more than 3,270 U.S. businesses were represented in Romania. Coca-Cola, Qualcomm, Citibank, McDonalds, and General Electric are some of the multinational corporations that are now operating in Romania. U.S. investors have shown interest Romania's electronics, transportation, chemical, mining, food, and banking sectors.

Below: In 2001, bilateral trade between the United States and Romania amounted to U.S. $895 million, which is nearly a 28 percent increase from the previous year.

Trade Relations with Canada

In January 2001, more than 700 Canadian companies were represented in Romania, and their combined investments amounted to a total of about U.S. $59 million. The two countries have established important joint ventures in the Romanian sectors of agriculture, banking, telecommunications, transportation, and tourism. In 2001, trade between the two countries totaled to about U.S. $67 million. Romania sold about U.S. $21 million worth of exports to Canada and imported about U.S. $ 46 million worth of Canadian goods. Romania exports mainly machinery, textiles, and consumer products, such as furniture and household items, to Canada and imports mainly machinery, electronic devices, and mineral products from Canada.

Since the early 1990s, both countries have shown strong support to each other in terms of economic development. Agencies such as the Romania-Canada Trade Economic Council, as well as the Canada-Romania Chamber of Commerce of Romania and the Export Development Corporation of Canada were set up to encourage and ensure a more fruitful trade relationship between the two nations. The Romanian Foreign Trade Center and the Trade Facilitation Office of Canada also help promote Romanian exports in Canada.

Above: The process of privatization has been slow but steady in Romania. In 2002, Romanian president Ion Iliescu went to Detroit, Michigan, on the last day of his official visit to the United States to meet with John Smith, the chairman of the board of directors at General Motors (GM). The purpose of their meeting was to discuss the possibility of GM taking over Romania's Electroputere electrical products factory in the city of Craiova.

Romanians in North America

In 2000, the United States was home to more than 397,500 people of Romanian ancestry. Of the Romanian Americans born outside of the United States, more than half arrived in the decade between 1980 and 1990. The largest Romanian communities in the United States can be found in California, New York, Florida, Michigan, and Ohio, where Romanians number in excess of 26,000. Smaller but significant populations of Romanians, ranging from 10,000 to 20,000 people, can be found in Illionis, New Jersey, and Pennsylvania. States with less than 10,000 Romanians include Arizona, Connecticut, Georgia, Indiana, Maryland, Massachusetts, Minnesota, Oregon, and Texas.

In Canada, Romanian immigrants arrived in several waves. The first Romanians to reach Canada were mostly Romanian Jews, who wanted to escape discrimination and persecution in nineteenth-century Romania. By the beginning of the 1900s, the Romanians who chose to settle in Canada were mostly farmers. Many were drawn by the Canadian government's program that allotted each adult immigrant a large plot of rural land to

Above: **The former coach of Nadia Comăneci, Bèla Karolyi is widely regarded as the most successful coach in the history of gymnastics. Today, he lives on a ranch near Houston, Texas, and trains aspiring U.S. gymnasts.**

develop. The conditions of the Canadian government's program were that the immigrants had to pay a relatively small fee and complete their development work, which included building a homestead and cultivating crops, in a span of three years. The Romanians who came to Canada after World War I were mostly skilled workers, academics, or professionals, many of whom, unlike their predecessors, settled in Canada's major cities. By 1989, the Canadian census reported that more than 70,000 ethnic Romanians were living in Canada, including large numbers in Toronto, Montreal, Hamilton, Edmonton, and Alberta. In the course of the 1990s, several thousand more Romanians immigrated to Canada.

Romanian restaurants are not uncommon in major U.S. and Canadian cities. Homesick Romanians and other Americans and Canadians visit them to get a taste of Romanian classics, such as sarmale, mămăliguţă, and tuică. Religion also plays a major role in bringing together Romanians in their new homelands. Numerous Romanian Orthodox churches exist in the United States and Canada. Today, many cultural institutions, such as the Romanian Museum in Philadelphia and the American Romanian Academy of Arts and Science in Montreal, and community groups, including the Romanian Medical Society in New York and the Romanians of Texas Association, operate in North America.

Left: Olympic gold medalist and gymnast Nadia Comăneci (*left*) is famous in North America in part because of her remarkable perfect-ten scores in the 1970s. She also helps run a prestigious gymnastics school, the Bart Conner Gymnastics Academy, located in Norman, Oklahoma. Comăneci married Bart Conner (*right*), also an Olympic gymnast, in 1996. Comăneci moved to the United States in 1989.

North Americans in Romania

Apart from government offices, North American presence in Romania today includes offices of the United States Agency for International Development (USAID), the Peace Corps, and the Canadian International Development Agency (CIDA) in Bucharest. Many North Americans in Romania also work for international aid agencies, such as World Vision, Save the Children, and UNICEF.

The first North Americans to reach Romania arrived in the mid-nineteenth century. Historically, most North Americans who ventured to Romania were merchants. They were attracted by the lucrative potential of the developing Romanian market and by the Romanian-made products they could take home to sell. By the end of the 1800s, Romania also hosted a handful of American oil-industry professionals. Romania's oil reserves are located near the Prahova River. In the period between the two world wars, some Americans saw industrially developing Romania as a land of business opportunities and set up companies and factories in the country.

Today, most North Americans enter Romania either as members of humanitarian organizations or as employees of large, multinational corporations that have offices in Romania. Significant communities of U.S. and Canadian businesspeople

Below: U.S. first lady Hillary Clinton tries to cheer up some HIV-positive children at the Ghoerge Lupu Hospital in Bucharest in 1996.

Above: **Romanian and U.S. soldiers unload equipment from a U.S. military airplane at the Mihail Kogalniceanu Airfield, near the city of Constanta. The soldiers are helping prepare Romania for the possible hosting of U.S. troops.**

live in Bucharest. Romania's mining, energy, and information technology sectors attract the most Canadians. A sizable number of North American doctors, mostly pediatricians, also visit Romania each year. Some of them work as volunteers in children's hospitals, while others give lectures on how to better care for Romania's enormous orphan population.

Various student- and teacher-exchange programs also draw a large number of North Americans to Romania. The Romanian Fulbright Commission is an important sponsor of such Romanian-American exchanges. The commission offers opportunities and scholarships to Romanian students who seek to pursue graduate studies in the United States and to American teachers, students, and researchers from the U.S. who would like to teach or work in Romania.

The United States and Canada are both represented by embassies in Bucharest. Michael Guest has been the U.S. ambassador to Romania since 2001, and Raphaël Girard has been the Canadian ambassador to Romania since 2000.

A   **B**   **C**   **D**

	National Boundary
	Provincial Boundary
■	Capital City
●	Major Town
	River
▲	Mountain
	Marshland

1

2

3

4

5

U K R A I N E

H U N G A R Y

SERBIA AND
MONTENEGRO

B U L G A R I A

Somes

Tisza

Tisza

SATU
MARE

MARMURES

Baia Mare

BIHOR

Oradea

SĂLAJ

CRISANA-
MARAMURES

Beiuş

CLUJ

Sic

Cluj-Napoca

ARAD

Mures

Roşia Montană

ALBA

Western Carpathians

TISZA PLAIN

TRANSYLVANIA

MURES

BISTRIŢA-
NĂSĂUD

SUCEAVA

Suceava

Dorohoi

BOTOŞANI

Siret

Cotnari

IAŞI

Iaşi

Prut

M

NEAMŢ

Eastern Carpathians

VASLUI

BACĂU

Oneşti

Siret

MOLDAVIA

GALAŢI

HARGHITA

Tarnave

SIBIU

Copşa Mica

Sibiu

BRAŞOV

COVASNA

VRANCEA

Gala

Timişoara

TIMIŞ

B A N A T

HUNEDOARA

Mount Moldoveanu
(8,347ft/2,544m)

▲

Southern Carpathians
(Transylvanian Alps)

Brasov

Bran

Căllmăneşti

Olt

Berca

BUZĂU

Buzău

BRĂILA

CARAS-SEVERIN

Hobitza

Tirgu Jiu

GORJ

MEHEDINTI

Craiova

VÎLCEA

ARGEŞ

Slatina

WALACHIA

Clejani

DIMBOVITA

Dealu Mare

PRAHOVA

Prahova

ILFOV

BUCHAREST

■

Murfatlar

IALOMITA

CĂLĂRAŞI

Danube

DOLJ

OLT

TELEORMAN

GIURGIU

Danube

86

Alba (county) B3–B4
Arad (county) A2–B3

Baia Mare B2
Bacău (county) C2–D3
Banat A3–B4
Beiuş B2
Berca D3
Bihor (county) A2–B3
Bistriţa-Năsăud
    B2–C2
Black Sea D5–E3
Botoşani (county) C2–D2
Brăila (county) D3–D4
Bran C3
Braşov C3
Braşov (county) C3
Bulgaria B4–E5
Bucharest C4–D4
Buzău D4
Buzău (county)C3–D4

Călăraşi (county) D4
Caraş-Şeverin (county)
    A3–B4
Clejani C4
Cluj (county) B2–B3
Cluj-Napoca B2
Constanţa E4
Constanţa (county)
    D4–E5
Copsa Mica C3
Covasna (county) C3–D3
Cotnari D2
Craiova B4
Crisana-Maramureş
    A2–B3

Danube (river) A3–E4
Danube Delta E3–E4
Dealu Mare C4–D4
Dimbovita (county)
    C3–C4
Dobruja D3–E4
Dolj (county) B4–C5
Dorohoi D2

Eastern Carpathians
    C2–C3

Galaţi D3
Galaţi (county) D3
Giurgiu (county) C5–D4
Gorj (county) B3–B4

Harghita (county) C2–D3
Hobitza B4
Hunedoara (county) B3
Hungary A1–A3

Ialomita (county) D4
Iaşi D2
Iaşi (county) D2
Ilfov (county) C4–D4

Above: **All decked out in colorful and richly embroided traditional costumes, these children are sharing a secret.**

Lake Razelm E4

Marmureş (county)
    B2–C2
Mehedinti (county) B4
Moldavia D1–D3
Moldova D1–E3
Moldoveanu C3
Movile Cave E4
Mureş (county) B3–C2
Mureş (river) A3–C3
Murfatlar D4

Neamţ (county) C2–D2

Olt (county) B4–C5
Olt (river) C2–C5
Oneşti D2–D3
Oradea B2

Prahova (county) C3–D4
Prahova River C3–D4
Prut (river) D1–D3

Roşia Montană B3

Satu Mare (county) B2
Serbia A3–B5
Serbia and Montenegro
    A3–B5

Sibiu C3
Sibiu (county) B3–C3
Sic B2
Siret (river) C1–D3
Slatina C4
Someş (river) B2–B3
Southern Carpathians
    B3–C3
Suceava D2
Suceava (county) C2–D2

Tărnave C3
Teleorman (county)
    C4–C5
Timiş (county) A3–B3
Timişoara A3
Tîrgu Jiu B4
Tisza (river) A3–C2
Tisza Plain A2–B4
Tulcea (county) D3–E4

Ukraine B1–E3

Vaslui (county) D2–D3
Vrancea (county) D3

Walachia B4–D4
Western Carpathians
    B2–B3

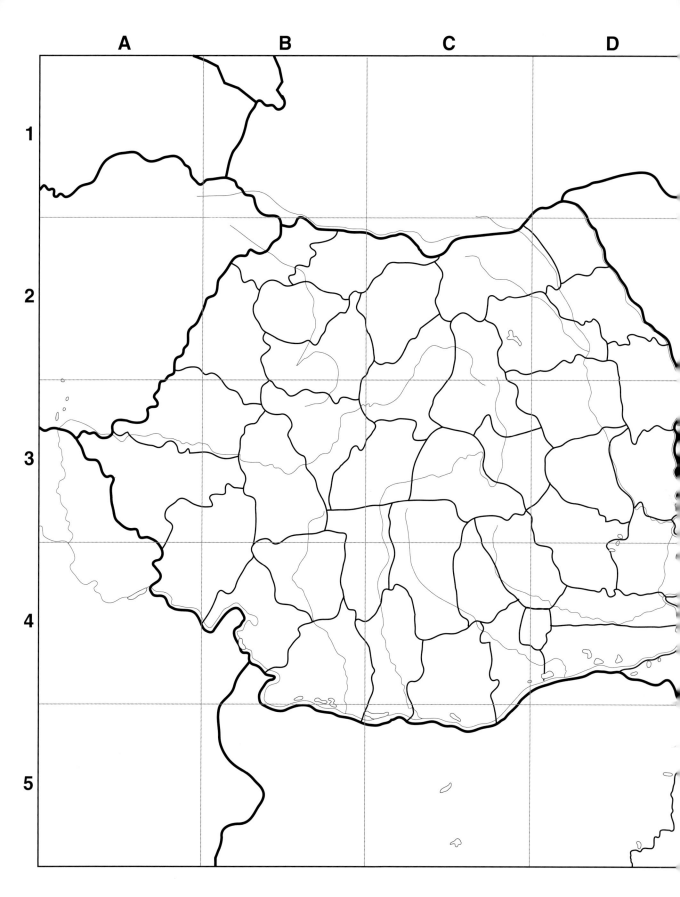

E

How Is Your Geography?

Learning to identify the main geographical areas and points of a country can be challenging. Although it may seem difficult at first to memorize the locations and spellings of major cities or the names of mountain ranges, rivers, deserts, lakes, and other prominent physical features, the end result of this effort can be very rewarding. Places you previously did not know existed will suddenly come to life when referred to in world news, whether in newspapers, television reports, other books and reference sources, or on the Internet. This knowledge will make you feel a bit closer to the rest of the world, with its fascinating variety of cultures and physical geography.

This map can be duplicated for use in a classroom. (PLEASE DO NOT WRITE IN THIS BOOK!) Students can then fill in any requested information on their individual map copies. The student can also make a copy of the map and use it as a study tool to practice identifying place names and geographical features on his or her own.

Below: With the Carpathian Mountains dominating the country's interior, Romania is home to numerous mountain villages.

Romania at a Glance

Official name   Romania

Capital   Bucharest

Official Language   Romanian

Population   22,317,730 (July 2002 estimate)

Land Area   91,675 square miles (237,500 sq km)

Administrative Regions   Alba, Arad, Argeş, Bacău, Bihor, Bistriţa-Năsaud, Botoşani, Brăila, Braşov, Bucharest (municipality), Buzău, Călăraşi, Caraş-Severin, Cluj, Constanţa, Covasna, Dîmboviţa, Dolj, Galaţi, Giurgiu, Gorj, Harghita, Hunedoara, Ialomita, Iaşi, Ilfov, Maramureş, Mehedinti, Mureş, Neamţ, Olt, Prahova, Sălaj, Satu Mare, Sibiu, Suceava, Teleorman, Timiş, Tulcea, Vaslui, Vîlcea, Vrancea.

Highest Point   Mount Moldoveanu 8,347 feet (2,544 m)

Major Rivers   Danube, Mureş, Olt, Prut, Siret, Someş

Major Mountain Ranges   Făgăras Range, Bucegi Range, Piatra Craiului Range, Retezat Range

Ethnic Groups   Romanians, Hungarians, Roma, Germans, Ukrainians

Main Religion   Romanian Orthodox Christianity

Major Festivals   Spring Amulet, Medieval Festival at Sighişoara, Easter, Christmas

Major Exports   textiles, footwear, metals and metal products, machinery and equipment, minerals

Major Imports   machinery and equipment, minerals and fuels, chemicals, consumer goods

Major Crops   wheat, corn, sugar beets, potatoes, grapes, sunflower seeds

Major Trade Partners   Italy, France, Germany, United Kingdom, United States.

Currency   Leu (34,100 Romanian Leu = U.S. $1 as of 2002)

Opposite: **The Putna Monastery is one of the finest examples of Romanian architecture.**

Glossary

Romanian Vocabulary

balmush (BAAL-mush): corn porridge with butter and cheese.

bulibasa (boo-lee-bah-SHAA): a chief of a Roma community.

Călușari (CAH-loo-shaah-ree): a mystical religious group in southern Romania; also the name of a famous dance performed by the group.

ciorba de burta (CHOWR-bah DE BOORD-tah): tripe soup.

ciorba de potroace (CHOWR-bah DE POH-trow-ah): turkey soup.

cobză (cob-ZAH): a stringed instrument that resembles a lute.

condei (KON-day): a sharp, penlike instrument used to etch color and intricate designs onto the shells of hard-boiled eggs.

dracul (DRAH-cool): devil or dragon.

Drăgaica (DRAH-GUY-kaah): an ancient rural festival celebrating harvest.

Hora (hoh-RAW): a traditional folk dance mostly by young men and women; sometimes performed by a newly married woman for good luck.

judete (joo-DEH-TSE): counties.

mămăliguță (MAAH-maah-lee-GOOH-tsah): corn porridge.

mititei (MEE-tee-tay): grilled sausages.

prefect (pre-FEHKT): the person who heads a county.

sarmale (SAAR-mah-leh): a traditional dish made of stuffing rolled in cabbage leaves.

Securitate (SEH-KOO-ree-TAH-teh): the Romanian secret police that operated during the communist period.

Sorcova (SOR-KOH-vaah): a traditional custom practiced on New Year's Eve.

stabor (staa-BORH): a Roma judge who helps settle disputes.

țambal (tsaam-BAAL): an instrument that resembles a cross between a guitar and a xylophone and is played using two small hammers to hit metal strings.

tuică (TSUI-ke): brandy typically made from plums.

English Vocabulary

accessible: easy to obtain or understand.

advocate: recommend, encourage, or support publicly.

Allies: the nations united against Germany and other Central Powers during World War I, first consisting of Great Britain, France, and Russia, and later joined by other countries, including the United States, Italy, and Japan.

autonomous: independent or having self-government.

capitulate: surrender to an enemy.

cardiovascular: related to or affecting the heart and blood vessels.

Council for Mutual Economic Assistance (COMECON): an organization set up and controlled by the Soviet Union to coordinate economic activity and roles between communist countries.

Crimean War: a war against Russia led by Great Britain, France, Turkey, and Sardinia (a Mediterranean island part of present-day Italy); the war was fought in Crimea, a peninsula in southeastern Ukraine on the Black Sea.

defect: to leave a cause or party, especially to join the opposition.

dissident: a person who disagrees with a government or a specific idea.

doctrine: teaching; ideas taught as principles of a religion.

Eastern Orthodox Church: a collective name for Orthodox churches that differ from the Roman Catholic Church by recognizing figures other than the Pope as the head of the church.

eclectic: wide-ranging; coming from many sources.

fortify: to make stronger; strengthen against attack.

intellectualism: devotion to the pursuit of intellectual or academic matters.

Gothic: related to a style of literature characterized by a gloomy setting and mysterious, sinister, or violent events.

grandeur: the quality of being grand; splendor and magnificence.

legacy: anything handed down from an ancestor.

medieval: from or characteristic of the Middle Ages, a period between the fifth and fifteenth centuries.

megalomaniac: a person who has delusions of personal grandeur and an obsession with doing extravagant things.

nationalistic: characterized by loyalty or devotion to a nation.

neurological: relating to a person's nervous system.

Neolithic: belonging to the New Stone Age period (8000–3500 B.C.); characterized by the use of polished stone tools, pottery, weaving, and agriculture.

pediatric: related to the branch of medicine concerned with the development, care, and diseases of children.

polygonal: describing shapes that have three or more sides.

principality: a territory that is governed by a prince.

prodigy: a child or young person who has extraordinary talent or ability.

pseudonym: a fictitious name used by an author to conceal his or her identity; pen name.

Romantic: of or relating to a style of literature and art that emphasizes emotions, the imagination, the ordinary person, and freedom of the spirit.

saline: related to the amount of salt contained in a body of water.

Sanskrit: an ancient Indian language.

synagogue: a place of worship and religious study for a Jewish community.

theologian: a specialist in the study of religion and the ways people of different religions relate themselves to God and the world around them.

unaffiliated: not connected with or belonging to a given group, organization, or movement.

Warsaw Pact: also known as the Warsaw Treaty Organization; an agreement made between communist nations in 1955.

More Books to Read

The Church of Orthodoxy. Religions of Humanity series. Olivier Clément (Chelsea House)

Communism. Political and Economic Systems series. David Downing and Richard Tames (Heinemann)

Eugene Ionesco. Bloom's Major Dramatists series. Robb Erskine (Chelsea House)

Gypsies. Endangered Cultures series. Elizabeth Sirimarco (Smart Apple Media)

Romania. Enchantment of the World series. Terri Willis (Children's Press)

Romania. Major World Nations series. Julian Popescu (Chelsea House)

Romania. Nations in Transition series. Mark Sanborne (Facts on File)

Top 10 Women Gymnasts. Sports Top 10 series. Septima Green (Enslow Publishers)

Videos

Ceauşescu: The Unrepentant Tyrant. Biography International series. (A & E Home Video)

Germany and Romania. Great Castles of Europe series. (Discovery Communication)

People Power: The End of Soviet-Style Communism. People's Century: Communism — The Promise and the Reality series. (WGBH Boston Video)

The Reshaping of a City/Rural Revival. Geographical Eye over Europe series. (ABC Video)

Web Sites

www.roembus.org

www.romania.org

www.rotravel.com

www.students.missouri.edu/~romsa/romania

www.turism.ro/english/index.php

Due to the dynamic nature of the Internet, some web sites stay current longer than others. To find additional web sites, use a reliable search engine with one or more of the following keywords to help you locate information about Romania. Keywords: *Bucharest, Carpathian Mountains, Nicolae Ceauşescu, Nadia Comăneci, Danube.*

Index

agriculture 5, 6, 9, 14, 18, 19, 38, 43, 82
Alba 70
Albania 28
Alexandrescu, Grigore 29
Antonescu, Ion 13
Arch of Triumph 13, 44
arts 14, 15, 27, 31, 35, 43, 45, 60, 61
Austria 12, 13
Austria-Hungary 12, 13
Austrians 12, 13, 50

Balkan Peninsula 5
Bessarabia 13
Black Sea 5, 6, 7, 9, 19, 34, 35, 41, 43, 79
Boulevard of Socialist Victory 5, 58, 59
Bran Castle 56, 57
Brancuşi, Constantin 60
Braşov 8, 21, 34, 38, 50, 51, 56
Bucharest 7, 8, 12, 17, 21, 25, 30, 31, 36, 38, 43, 44, 45, 48, 58, 61, 66, 77
Bukovina 13, 30
Bulgaria 6, 7, 11, 28
Buzău 6, 64

Călusari 27, 46, 47
Canada 36, 54, 75, 78, 79, 81, 82, 83, 84
Canada-Romania Chamber of Commerce 81
Carpathian Mountains 5, 6, 7, 9, 10, 19, 34, 43, 62, 64, 79
caves 7, 48, 49
Ceauşescu, Nicolae 14, 17, 30, 43, 44, 45, 58, 59, 66, 67, 72, 73, 80

chamois 9
children 21, 22, 23, 40, 52, 72, 73, 84, 85
climate 8
Clinton, Hillary 84
Cluj-Napoca 21, 48
Comăneci, Nadia 36, 54, 55, 83
communism 5, 13, 14, 18, 19, 35, 52, 53, 66, 67, 77
Constanţa 21, 27
Constantinescu, Emil 78
Constantinople 11
Copsa Mica 52, 53
Council for Mutual Economic Assistance (COMECON) 14
Covasna 8
Craiova 21, 25, 81
Crisana-Maramureş 7

Dacians 10, 11, 31, 70, 71
dancing 38, 46, 47
Danube Delta 7, 9, 19, 53
Danube River 5, 6, 7, 18, 41, 43, 52, 53
democracy 5, 13, 14, 16, 77
Dobruja 6, 7, 8, 19, 20
Dracula 29, 43, 56, 57
dual monarchy (*see* Austria-Hungary)

Eastern Orthodox Christianity 11, 12, 26, 69, 83
economy 5, 13, 14, 17, 18, 19, 70, 77, 80, 81
education 34, 35
Eliade, Mircea 28, 43, 61
Enesco, Georges 28, 32, 43, 61
Europe 5, 6, 8

European Union (EU) 53

fascism 13
family 22, 34
festivals 38, 39, 43, 50, 51
flag 5
food 39, 40, 41
forests 9, 19, 34
France 5

Galaţi 21, 53
gender 20, 21, 22, 23, 33
geography 5, 6, 7, 35, 43, 62, 63, 64, 65
Germans 13, 20, 26, 27
Germany 13, 18, 75
Gheorghiu-Dej, Gheorghe 14
government 5, 10, 11, 12, 13, 14, 15, 16, 17, 18, 20, 23, 24, 52, 53, 58, 59, 69, 73, 75, 76, 77, 78, 79, 82
Greeks 10, 11, 28
gross domestic product (GDP) 17, 18
Groza, Petru 13, 14
gymnastics 36, 37, 54, 55, 82, 83

handicrafts 33, 37, 39
Harghita 8
House of the People (*see* Palace of Parliament)
Hunedoara 10
Hungarians 5, 11, 13, 20, 24, 26, 27, 50
Hungary 6, 7, 11, 12, 13, 53

Iaşi 21, 30
Iliescu, Ion 14, 15, 16, 75, 78, 81
industry 14, 18, 19, 52, 53, 79, 84

International Monetary Fund (IMF) 18
Ionesco, Eugene 28, 31, 43, 61
Iron Guard 13
Islam 27

Jews 27, 82

Karolyi, Bela 54, 82
Khrushchev, Nikita 14
kings
  Béla IV 27
  Carol I 12, 15, 26
  Charlemagne 11
  Ferdinand I 13, 15
  Matthias Corvinus 57

Lake Razelm 7
language 10, 24, 25, 28, 29, 31, 61, 69
literature 27, 29, 57

marriage 21, 22
Medieval Art Festival 35
Micu-Klein, Ion Inochentie 12
military service 17, 22, 67
mineral springs 34, 62, 63
Moldavia 5, 6, 7, 8, 9, 11, 12, 15, 30, 38
Moldova 6, 7, 13
Movile Cave 7, 48, 49
Muddy Volcanoes 6, 64, 65
music 32, 38

Nastase, Adrian 16
Nastase, Ilie 37
National Salvation Front (NSF) 14
North Atlantic Treaty Organization (NATO) 14, 77, 78
nuclear power 79

oil 19, 84

Olympic Games 37, 54, 55, 76
Ottoman Turks 5, 11, 12, 15, 28, 29, 50, 56, 57

Palace of Parliament 17, 30, 43, 58, 59
Palade, George Emil 83
pollution 18, 52, 53
princes
  Carol I 12, 15
  Alexandru Cuza 12
  Michael the Brave 15
  Stephen the Great 15, 26, 30
  Vlad the Impaler (see Vlad Ţepeş)

queens
  Elizabeth 15
  Marie 15
  Victoria 15

religion 11, 12, 26, 27, 39, 46, 61, 69, 71, 83
religious architecture 26, 27, 30, 44, 45, 59
revolution 14, 66, 67
Roma 20, 24, 68, 69
Roman Catholicism 11, 12, 26, 27
Romanian Academy 28
Romanian Communist Party 14, 17, 67
rural life 21, 29, 32, 35
Russia 12, 13, 27, 54
Russians 12

Sarmizegetusa 10, 70, 71
seasons 8, 38
Securitate 14, 66
Sibiu 66
Sighişoara 35
Slavs 10, 11
soccer 36
Soviet Union 13, 14, 76

sports 34, 35, 36, 37, 54, 55
Stalin, Joseph 14
Stoker, Bram 29, 56, 57
Suceava 30
Sylva, Carmen (see Queen Elizabeth)

Ţepeş, Vlad 15, 29, 43, 44, 56, 57
theater 28, 31, 35
Timişoara 14, 66, 67
Tisza River 53
Tisza Plain 7, 13
Tokes, Laszlo 66
tourism 19, 34, 35
traditions 21, 27, 38, 39, 46, 47, 50, 51, 61
Transylvania 5, 6, 7, 11, 12, 14, 15, 20, 27, 30, 56, 57
Treaty of Küçük Kaynarca 12
Tzara, Tristan 60

Ukraine 6, 13
unemployment 13, 18, 23
United Nations (UN) 52
United States 36, 61, 75, 76, 77, 80, 82, 83, 84, 85
universities 25
U.S. presidents
  George W. Bush 75, 77
  Bill Clinton 77
  Richard Nixon 76

vineyards 19, 40
Voroneţ Monastery 26

Walachia 5, 6, 7, 8, 9, 11, 12, 15, 30, 44, 56, 57
Warsaw Pact 14, 76
World War I 5, 13, 15, 28, 29, 43, 44, 75, 82, 83, 84
World War II 13, 28, 29, 43, 44, 84

Yugoslavia 6, 28, 53